Joy My
710 South Fi~~nal Street~~
Lafayette, IN 47905
(765) 742-2102

GET
A
LIFE

How to Leave That Dead-End Job Behind and Create Your Perfect Future – *Today!*

DO YOU OWN YOUR LIFE ... ?

Do you already own a business? Have you ever considered the possibility of starting one? Either way, this book is for you. Today, Network Marketing may be the only way for you to create true wealth and financial independence.

Get A Life! will show you how to create a large, permanent, royalty income by getting involved with an exciting Network of people and sharing a unique and explosive business idea.

Philip Stills is an entrepreneur with 25 years of education and experience in traditional business, including real estate investing, franchising, chain stores, and managing employees. His passion for developing successful, small businesses brought him to Network Marketing in 1989.

Get A Life! is the result of over five years of hands-on experience in developing his own international Network Marketing business, along with literally thousands of hours of intense study with successful leaders in the industry.

The book teaches you an Eight-Step Success System that anyone can duplicate and that has been used successfully by thousands of people in many countries. You need just a little time and a small amount of money to get started. No experience is required. Network Marketing is a business open to anyone who is ready to learn and wants to succeed.

If you are looking for a proven way to create a more abundant life—one that provides you with true wealth, financial independence and personal time freedom—this book shows how Network Marketing can take you there.

Get a life! Start creating your future right away.

Read the first chapter tonight.

What Network Marketing leaders say about this book...

"Interesting. Thorough. Easy to read and to the point. This book is definitely on my list of suggested reading."

—Doris Wood, President, MLMIA
(MultiLevel Marketing International Association)

"The book has a natural rhythm and an easiness of comprehension that would serve well both beginners and seasoned veterans of this industry."

—J.F. Robert Bolduc, President, Matol Botanical International, Inc.

"I agree that the 1990s will be a time for individuals to venture into new ways of improving their quality of life, both personally and professionally. Network Marketing is one way of doing this and becoming financially independent at the same time."

—Damon DeSantis, President, Rexall Showcase International

"You are responsible for creating your life and your future."

—Brian Tracy, author, *Maximum Achievement*

"Your thoughts create either prosperity or scarcity in your life. Your thoughts create your life."

—Dr. Wayne W. Dyer, author, *Real Magic*

"I never got anywhere or made any money watching television."

—Philip Stills, author, *Get A Life!*

What business experts say about Network Marketing....

"The vertical to horizontal power shift that Networks bring about will be enormously liberating for individuals. Hierarchies promote moving up and getting ahead, producing stress, tension, and anxiety. Networking empowers the individual and people in the Networks to nurture one another."
— John Naisbitt, futurist and author

"A Network is the exact opposite of a bureaucracy. In a bureaucracy, the purpose is to collect power and distribute it down through a flow chart of underlings. In a Network, the purpose is to give power away. Many businesses are starting to Network. The essence of the recent trend, described in the fastest-selling business books, is to develop a win/win approach, to forget about your own quotas, to focus exclusively on how best to serve people."
— Dr. Wayne Dyer, psychologist and author

"In most firms, work is a job. But in Network Marketing organizations, the company offers a mission and a way of life. Network Marketing revives the life-and-work style of the American frontier, when the family unit and economic unit were the same thing. Unlike a job, a Network Marketing business is founded explicitly on character, values and American free enterprise."
— Nicole Woolsey Biggart, professor of management and sociology

"That's why I am attracted to businesses such as Amway and Mary Kay. For little or nothing down, you can be in business around the world—if you're willing to persevere and work harder than the competition."
— Newt Gingrich, U.S. Senator

"You become what you think about."
— Earl Nightingale, author, *The Essence of Success*

"One of the most valuable things you can learn is the art of using the knowledge and experience of others."
— Napolean Hill, author, *Law of Success*

"The more advanced the technology for delivery and home shopping, the more people need Network Marketing . . . It has carved out the essence, or the best part of retailing—educating people about products and services that will improve their lives and that they don't yet know exist—and that's what Network Marketing today is really all about."

—Paul Zane Pilzer, economist and author

"Network Marketing takes the frustration out of buying. People hate waiting in line. Nobody wants to go to stores anymore. As the person-to-person deliverers get classier, better and more trusted, everything—from baskets to insurance—will be sold interactively, person-to-person . . . the retail environment is going to just have to close up. Nobody wants to go there. And Network Marketing has the solution."

—Faith Popcorn, futurist and author

"It is natural to cling to security. It's the type of security you are clinging to that makes the difference. Static security is clinging to a branch over a torrent of water, praying that the branch won't break. It's a kind of false security. Dynamic security is learning how to swim. Today, it's the only kind of security. And it's what Network Marketing offers."

—Scott DeGarmo, editor and publisher

"Network Marketing is the most powerful way to reach consumers in the 90's."

—Richard Poe, editor and author

"The best use of capital is in the hands of the many. And that's why Network Marketing is the greatest source of grassroots capitalism. You learn how to take a small bit of capital, which is time, and a small bit of capital, which is money, and start the American dream process right from the grass roots."

—Jim Rohn, speaker and author

Upline™ Press
Charlottesville, Virginia

Cover and Diagrams by Luke Melia; Book Design by John David Mann

Upline™ Press books may be purchased for educational, business, or sales promotional use. For information: Upline™ Press, 400 East Jefferson Street, Charlottesville, Virginia 22902 (804) 979-4427 fax (804) 979-1602.

Second Edition

Library of Congress Cataloging-in-Publication Data
Stills, Philip
    Get A Life! / Philip Stills
    p. 208 cm.
    ISBN 0-9634259-2-7
    1. Success-Time aspects 2. Achievement 3. Motivation 4. Self-actualization
    I. Title

ACKNOWLEDGMENTS

This book took a long time to write.

Many, many people helped along the way, and I am especially grateful to those who read it and used it and made suggestions for its improvement during its various, previous forms.

Bev Johnson and Jim Floor of the International Networking Association (INA) deserve a great deal of credit for much of the material in this book, because they taught me most of what I know and have shared with you in this book. I spent countless hours with them as they patiently explained Network Marketing to me.

Why did it take me so long to get it?

Because I am not the brightest student in the world—and because I didn't have a book like this to lay it all out, step by step, in plain American. Now, you will learn as much in one weekend from this book as I learned in five years of driving to seminars, participating in meetings and actually building the business hands-on.

This project became a book thanks to Bernard Shir-Cliff, literary agent, editor, and publisher's consultant.

I owe a phenomenal debt to a great many people for their leadership and inspiration in an exciting new industry.

Thank you, Rich DeVos of Amway Corporation, Mary Kay Ash of Mary Kay Cosmetics, Scott DeGarmo of *Success* magazine, Brian Tracy of Brian Tracy International, Doris Wood of MultiLevel Marketing International Association (MLMIA), Blake Roney of Nu Skin International Inc., J.F. Robert Bolduc of Matol Botanical International, Inc., Damon DeSantis of Rexall Showcase International, James Preston of Avon Products Inc., Arthur R. Bauer of American Media Inc., Jay Martin of NSA, and so many others that I cannot begin to list them.

For this "new and improved" revision of *Get A Life!*, my thanks to Randolph Byrd, President and Publisher of *Upline*™ Press and MLM Publishing, Inc., and his partner, editor John Milton Fogg

To Rana and Kendra,
that you may create freedom and independence when you are young
and live your own rich life of abundance and wealth.

CONTENTS

WHO SHOULD READ THIS BOOK . . . .

Are you interested in protecting your life's single most important *investment?*

Is your goal to have more money and the time to really, freely *enjoy it?*

If you answered "Yes" to these two questions, there's one more I need to ask you:

Do you know how *to do these things, right now—today?*

This book is about protecting your investment in *your future.*

This book is about your earning more money—perhaps a lot more money.

Even more important, it's about your having the time you desire and deserve to thoroughly enjoy all the money you've earned!

And finally, this book will show you how to begin doing that—*today*—in a proven and very powerful way.

This is a book about Network Marketing, an exciting new career choice that can make you rich and free in the next two to five years.

Now, I'm not saying it will be easy.

I *am* saying that *you* can do it—and, that if you simply do what this book teaches, you will succeed.

Obviously, I can't "guarantee" your success. Nobody else can, either, for that matter. Your success is up to you.

But *I can guarantee* this: The book you're holding in your hands will deliver on its promise of showing you what *you need to do* to become successful in Network Marketing. And I do mean *guarantee:*

Get A Life! comes with an absolutely sincere 100 percent money-back guarantee: If, for any reason, you do not get all the value you expect from reading this book and from applying what you learn from it, the publisher will give you a full, no-questions-asked refund. Is that fair?

Here's another good reason to read this book: If you *don't* read it, the chances are better than good that five years from now, you'll still be in the same place where you are today—making the same money, doing the same things, driving the same car, and the rest. (Except everything will cost a lot more.)

This book can change that.

There are only three ways I know of to make money. You can:

1) TRADE YOUR TIME FOR DOLLARS ... in which case you will always run out of time and your income will plateau and eventually grow smaller.

2) LEVERAGE YOUR EXTRA MONEY ... (if you have any) in investments such as stocks and real estate. But most people are not expert at doing that and lose money that way.

Or ...

3) LEVERAGE YOUR TIME ... You can create more money by investing a little bit of that time in other people.

Number three certainly seems the best choice ... but how do I do that?"

There are four ways you *could* leverage your time. The first three you'll recognize easily; the fourth may be less familiar to you than the others:

1) Hiring employees;

2) Opening retail or chain stores;

3) Franchising;

4) Network Marketing.

Network Marketing, the fourth way to leverage your time, is the simplest and most powerful way to get into business and create sales revenue and profits in the marketplace. Although it is not yet that well or widely understood, it is fast exploding as one of the most exciting and profitable ways to reach consumers with products and services, internationally, without the crushing overhead expenses, frustrations and limitations of conventional "business as usual."

I predict (and I am joined by a rapidly growing group of business experts like Paul Pilzer, Faith Popcorn, Scott DeGarmo and Brian Tracy) that someday, Network Marketing *will* be "business as usual." But that's not how it is today—not yet.

And that is good news for you.

That means that right now, you have an unprecedented *window of opportunity*. If you get involved in Network Marketing *now*, mastering the principles and building a strong foundation for your own Networking business as quickly as possible, then when the masses come on board, you'll be in the best possible place to capitalize on your investment, reaping rich and long-lasting rewards.

Millions of people are now involved; *hundreds of millions* will be involved before long.

You see, today you have to think differently about what it is to work, to earn money, to have a job. The world has changed.

Today, you have to *create your own financial future.*

So how do I do that?!

Network Marketing—that's how

Get A Life! will put you in complete creative control of your future with a mature and proven business concept that literally knows no limits . . . a business idea that has been legal and successful since the mid-1940s and is just now emerging widely as the answer to the limitations of retailing, franchising and all the growing problems of doing business with employees, by mail order, in malls, stores and chains.

Again, please understand: *Network Marketing is not well understood by most people.*

It's a lot like the position the franchising industry held in the late 1960s; people at the time thought franchising was a pyramid scam and a rip-off— it had a terrible image. Big corporations wouldn't even use the word "franchise" in their opportunity ads 30 years ago. And look at the industry now! Franchising is all around us. Franchising is responsible for over one third of all sales of *everything* in the U.S.! Vast fortunes have been made through franchising, and it has become a staple feature of our business scenery.

However, if you want to go out and actually start a successful franchise yourself, you need *a lot* of startup money; the average cost of a franchise is upwards of $85,000! You also need a lot of business experience to succeed in franchising today. In fact, a third of all franchises fail; another third break even; and only one third ever make a profit.

Network Marketing, which today still experiences some of the same slow acceptance as franchising did thirty years ago, starts where franchising leaves off.

Through Network Marketing, men and women just like you are creating fortunes—both in money, and in terms of *personal time.* Brave individuals who have taken the time to learn what Network Marketing really is and how they can use it to create the life they want are having phenomenal success! And the best part is that you can get into Network Marketing with very little money (I'm talking hundreds of dollars) and with very little time (hours per week—not days), and the best part is that you have a *proven* success system to duplicate; you don't need to figure it out, you simply need to do it

Forget about re-inventing the wheel. Just do the things that work. And that's what *getting a life* is all about!

Do you already know something about Network Marketing? If so, I have a request:

Whatever you know, or *assume* you know, put it aside for just a moment. What you are about to discover will surprise you in a very good way.

And if you don't already have the life and work you truly want . . . just read the first chapter.

ABOUT THE AUTHOR

Philip Stills is an entrepreneur with experience in each of the four ways to leverage time in business.

In the 1970s, his family owned a chain of vacation resorts in Northern California, and that's where he got his experience with the frustrations of hiring employees and managing chain locations.

In the 1980s, he owned a large video store franchise and became all too familiar with the limitations of the franchise industry. In the 1990s, he created a Network Marketing business, which he is excitedly expanding internationally.

After an exhaustive study of the Network Marketing industry, he developed an Eight-Step—no-limit—Success System for leveraging time to the fullest and for creating unlimited residual income.

He is also a real estate broker and investor, and he owns a real estate finance business.

Philip Stills has business degrees in both marketing and real estate.

He lives in Santa Rosa, California, with his wife and two daughters and his dog, a Chesapeake Bay Retriever that would rather fetch and swim than anything else. Philip Stills would rather ski in deep powder at Alpine Meadows or Alta than practically anything else.

He would make a very good friend.

CHAPTER 1
A Glimmer of Hope

G*et A Life!* is about creating a life with both time and money. This book will teach you how to leverage your time. This book will teach you how to create a large residual income without interfering with your present job or business.

Note that term "residual"—that is the key that creates the *leverage.* So what is "residual income"? It's like royalties: authors, musicians, actors and inventors receive residual income long after they perform the work for which they're being paid. Residual income is *money that keeps coming to you long after you have completed the initial work.*

Most of us have never considered the possibility that we, too, can create and enjoy royalties on our past efforts. Yet that possibility is very real; in fact, as you read these lines, hundreds of thousands of individuals without the special talents or skills of an artist are living exciting, fulfilling lives fueled by the time and money created through residual income. The purpose of this book is to help you become one of those people.

This book is about a business idea that *you* can use to create your own lasting residual income—and you don't need much time or money to get started. Anybody can learn to do it, and do it quickly and easily, too.

You have time—all the time you need; it's just a matter of knowing your priorities and leveraging your time with the best financial vehicle for you.

You don't need to be gifted or talented—or even lucky.

You don't need a college degree or a particularly outgoing or aggressive personality.

You simply need a little bit of time and a small amount of money to get started.

You just need to be yourself, and be willing to work hard for something you want badly—whether it's spiritual or material, for yourself or for others, or all of the above.

And, you've got to grab hold of some important ideas that might seem to be upside down or even impossible at first.

Financial advisors recommend that you pay yourself first—putting away 10 percent of every dollar you earn for your future. Eventually, over years, your savings will compound and grow and start paying you interest. Then, you start earning interest on the interest. This widely understood concept of putting your money to work for you is called leveraging. Leveraging money is the central idea behind all great fortunes.

But few people understand that you also need to leverage 10 percent of your *time* for your future.

When you leverage your time, you create more time—"interest on your time," so to speak—*and* you automatically create more money, too.

You have 168 hours a week. That's what everyone has. Ten percent of that number is about 16 hours. And since the average American adult watches 27 hours of television, that's less time than most people waste with remote in hand each and every week!

Most people spend at least the 16 hours you need to leverage in pursuit of unproductive activities that are *tension relieving*, but not *goal achieving*.

Get A Life! will teach you how to leverage your time, so you can live your life precisely the way you've always imagined it could be, but were unable to do until now.

That's what I mean by *Getting A Life!*: living your life as if it were an unfolding artistic masterpiece.

When you are *Getting A Life,* you will enter an enchanted world where you can direct the unfolding scenes that you call your life.

We human beings are happiest when we feel that we have some creative control of our lives. When we believe that we can influence our future, even for just an instant, we enjoy freedom, confidence and peace of mind.

This book is unlike any other book that you have ever picked up. A bold claim? Perhaps—but by the time you finish this first chapter, I'm guessing that you will see why I make it.

Get A Life! is not another exercise in positive thinking, nor is it a recital of correct, self-talk affirmations.

It is not a collection of instant techniques to produce friends and influence people.

It is not a motivational presentation to get you hyped on the possibility of your success, either.

Those positive, self-talk affirmations, motivational raps and the rest are short-term "feel goods" and cannot by themselves sustain your enthusiasm because they are external techniques. I'm not putting down "people skills" or external motivation. They are valuable, but they don't fundamentally show you what to do to change the situation. They are useless to you unless you have a long-term plan and a financial vehicle for leveraging your time and your life.

This book is about being on the leading edge of tomorrow's trends and social impulses *today*, about not being left behind financially. It will teach some solid concepts that may, at first, seem strange; ideas like residual income, duplication of effort, time leveraging, romancing your future, and personal freedom.

These concepts are instruments for the long haul. The book will give you some practical tools that will make it easy for you to get from where you are today to where you want to be socially and financially in two to five years.

So, stick with it. Be open to the new ideas you learn here. Try them on like shoes. If they fit—buy them, and walk in them anywhere you want to go!

This book will also teach you how simple it is to make money and save money when you have the right financial vehicle to begin with. The exciting news is that you can change and grow right now. You can change your limiting thoughts about time and money and your future today.

People tell me, "I'm doing okay."

I say, "Compared to what ... to the life you want? Compared to whom ... to your family? Your neighbors? Your peers at work?"

"Hey, they're all broke!"

Conformity will keep you broke. Comparison leads to failure.

How would you choose to live if money were no problem ... ?

What kind of house would you live in ... ?

Which neighborhood ... ?

What kind of cars would you drive ... ?

What charities would you support with your time ... ?

What causes would you support with your money ... ?

What kinds of vacations would you take ... ? Would it be exciting to take a real vacation this year instead of visiting the relatives again?

How do you *really* want to live?

What would you be doing *right now* if you were living that way ... ?

If you had the time and the money, *you would live differently.* And if you had residual income, you would have the time and the money to do it.

And here's the key, which seems so simple, yet few people fully grasp it: *To live differently, you need to do something fundamentally different.* This little vignette shows you what I mean:

I'm sitting in a quiet room at the Millcroft Inn, a peaceful little place hidden back among the pine trees about an hour out of Toronto. It's just past noon, late July—and I'm listening to the desperate sounds of a life-or-death struggle going on just a few feet away.

There's a small fly burning out the last of its short life's energies in a futile attempt to fly through the glass of the windowpane. The winning wings tell the poignant story of the fly's strategy—try harder.

But it's not working.

The frenzied effort offers no hope for survival. Ironically, the struggle is part of the trap. It is impossible for the fly to try hard enough to succeed at breaking through the glass. Nevertheless, this little insect has staked its life on reaching its goal through raw effort and determination.

This fly is doomed. It will die there on the windowsill.

Across the room, ten steps away, the door is open. Ten seconds of flying time and this small creature could reach the outside world it seeks. With only a fraction of the effort now being wasted, it could be free of this self-imposed trap. The breakthrough possibility is there. It would be so easy.

Why doesn't the fly try another approach, something dramatically different? How did it get so locked in on the idea that this particular route, and determined effort, offer the most promise for success? What logic is there in continuing until death, to seek a breakthrough with "more of the same"?

No doubt this approach makes sense to the fly. Regrettably, it's an idea that will kill.

"Trying harder" isn't necessarily the solution to achieving more. It may not offer any real promise for giving what you want out of life. Sometimes, in fact, it's a big part of the problem.

—Price Pritchett, Ph.D.

An open mind is necessary for growth. An open mind is positive. Like a parachute, it only works when it is open. I want you to fully comprehend that if you keep doing what you are doing—even if, *especially* if you "try harder"—you will keep getting more of the same results.

Here's a definition of insanity I've heard that speaks volumes about the way people live and work in today's world:

Insanity is when you keep doing the same things over and over and expect to produce different results.

Sowing and reaping. Cause and effect.
Want different effects? Try some different causes.
Thoughts are causes. Your life is the effect.
There is no reason for you to die like that fly.

I've had to grow a lot in my life and work.

I once thought the way to succeed was to get a good education, and then get a good job, and then work hard until someone—my boss—recognized my effort and rewarded my achievement, so I could buy the things that would tell other people (and myself) that I was successful. I wanted status.

I didn't realize that I had put my future under someone else's control. I let someone else tell me how much I was worth. Someone else decided what kind of car I drove, what kind of house I lived in, how much money I could save, what time I had to get up in the morning—everything.

I gave away my freedom.

Hey, that's what everyone else was doing, and I just figured, "That's how the system works." But I wasn't really thinking about what happened to all the people who went down the same path before me.

A French entomologist lined up a bunch of Processionary Caterpillars on the rim of a clay flower pot. This type of caterpillar is known for its following instinct: these caterpillars always follow each other, traveling in lines, end to end to end.

The entomologist's caterpillars formed an unbroken circle around the rim of the pot, tip to tail. They followed each other around and around for seven days and seven nights, nonstop. One by one they dropped off the flowerpot and died from sheer exhaustion.

The amazing thing was that even though they had plenty of food and water within easy reach, their instinct for following was so strong not one of them broke ranks to eat, drink, or sleep. There was not one leader in the bunch. They followed each other into oblivion.

You can find out where your life is headed by taking a look at the people who are ten years ahead of you in your career or your business.

How do they live . . . ?

Do they have the life you want . . . ?

Maybe so. Usually not.

I reached a point where I realized that I did not want to die like a Processionary Caterpillar.

What I saw was that the people who were one decade ahead of me were burned out. They were not rich and free. They had plateaued: their incomes had leveled off; their *lives* had leveled off. In some cases their incomes and lives were going down! They were no longer excited—and weren't very exciting either.

I knew I did not want what they had. And I wanted what they didn't have. I had to learn to say "No."

I was lucky. I found the open door to a beautiful, bright future. I quit banging my head on the glass ceiling. (Yes, there's one in place for men, too.) I was lucky because my parachute happened to work: my mind happened to be open when I was introduced to these new ideas. I flew toward freedom. I learned how to leverage my time, and today I'm *owning my future*.

You can do it, too.

Now I have more time to do the things that make me happy, such as enjoying time with my wife and two beautiful daughters. We're debt-free with an expanding income. We're both full-time parents. We're able to buy and do many of the things today that were only dreams two to five years ago.

We found an exciting financial vehicle that allowed us to escape the vagaries of our own real estate finance company and the uncertainties of national and world economies. We were earning a six-figure income in our own mortgage business, and we looked real good on paper, but there was no security . . . no time and few friends.

Now, we have hundreds of friends.

Now, we have the time.

As a typical owner of a small, traditional business, my income was limited by my own efforts. I was not leveraging my time. My income was limited by the number of hours in the day. My income was only as secure as my last deal, because I never knew where the next transaction would come from. Other people and circumstances beyond my control determined my future.

I needed to control my own future.

I was intensely interested in learning more about this unique concept of leveraging time. Somehow, I had to get control of my income and my financial future. I wanted to be free, with both my time and my money. I wanted the security of residual income. I wanted my freedom!

I wanted to become involved in something bigger than myself, something with stability and unlimited potential for growth and income.

Another animal story, this time about some fascinating research with rats.

One scientist took a healthy young rat from its cage every day and dropped it into a barrel of water. It could not get out. The rat had to swim and swim and swim, and there was no way it could rest. When it became so exhausted that it was on the verge of sinking and drowning, the scientist rescued it and returned it to its cage, until the next day's torture session.

Every day the rat endured this extreme anxiety.

After several weeks of this terrifying abuse, the rat was killed and dissected. This once young and vigorous rat displayed all the physical characteristics of an old and decrepit rat. The muscle fiber and the tissues were physically aged and visibly distressed. The once supple young rat had become a rigid old rat, with tough, inflexible, darkened flesh.

The cause?

Worrying. The unrelenting stress of his daily life.

The tedious, daily job routine of most people is like being dropped day after day into a barrel of water with no way out and no place to rest. It's panic. It's a meaningless life for many people. An existence without recognition, without dignity, without creativity, without any sense of accomplishment. An existence with little or no reward.

The Bureau of Labor Statistics reports that 81 percent of all working Americans hate their jobs, but do not have the guts (or is it the opportunity?) to quit and change. This turns vigorous young people into diseased old people, slowly but very, very surely.

It's like boiling a frog.

They say if you drop a frog into a pot of boiling water, he'll leap right out. But if you place him gently into warm water, he likes it, and then you slowly bring the water to a boil and he doesn't even notice that he's getting cooked until it's too late. You might be getting cooked, slowly, just by getting used to the heat and the pressure of life and—along with almost everybody else—not knowing you can do anything about it.

There's a story about the farm animals arguing one evening. The horse was bragging how far he had traveled that day. The dog insisted that he had run farther. The ox claimed that he had gone the farthest, because he had been walking all day since sunrise.

The ox was right, in a sense—but in truth he hadn't gone anywhere at all, except in circles in the same rut, yoked to a spoke, turning a wheel on a gear which caused some effect in a system he did not even begin to understand.

The purpose of this book is to help you change the way you think about making money and to alter some of the oppressive and self-limiting ideas you may have about owning your own business. You *can* own your own Network Marketing business, and you can get started with very little time and very little money.

Maybe you don't accept that possibility.

Maybe you don't want it yet.

Maybe you are afraid of the idea.

Well, keep reading, and your open mind will parachute you into some exciting new terrain where the brilliant horizon will dawn on you clearly, spectacularly, and you will know that you *have* to own a Network Marketing business if you want to live the way you dream of living.

You need to own a source of residual income to become rich and free—financially independent and personally free, whatever that means to you.

Not just any business will do it, certainly not "business as usual." You'll need an independent, high-leverage business.

The alternative to owning a no-limit business is to give up on your dreams and shrink your goals when your income levels off at your job or in your traditional business. You will plateau; that's a foregone conclusion. It's just a matter of when.

But you *can* own a business that will allow you to increase your income to match your goals. This unique business concept will teach you to own your future and to dream as big as you can. You will learn how to leverage time without disturbing your present income situation.

Anyone can learn how to succeed. You don't need any special experience.

This book will teach you everything you need to know to get started.

This book will help you find the right people who are willing and able to help you succeed. You can find the small amount of time and money needed to get started. Anyone can do it—*anyone!*

Again: This book is not about "business as usual." I'm not talking about having a store or office with employees, inventory, equipment, overhead and capital requirements.

It's not about selling door-to-door or having parties in your home to sell products to friends.

We're not talking about some little mail order business that you run from your kitchen table.

We're not talking about operating a mini-mart in your garage.

We're not talking about product demonstrations or a delivery route.

None of those things.

You don't need to be a salesperson. You just need to be yourself.

You need to know what you want, and you need to want it badly enough to commit to follow a proven success system, work hard for your goal and never give up.

You need to learn to like yourself and other people.

You need to work on getting rid of fear and doubt by improving your self-image.

This book will teach you an exciting business idea that is practically invisible—a business that exists and expands primarily in the minds of ambitious people, a business that can create an enormous volume of products and services worldwide through a Network of people.

It is a business that can make you rich and free in two to five years, part-time, without any of the drawbacks of an ordinary enterprise.

This book is about Network Marketing—a simple yet remarkably powerful form of business that organizes people positively for mutual profit in a revolutionary way.

Network Marketing is a modern business concept that is as fresh and exciting today in the Nineties as the business concept of franchising was in the Sixties.

Franchising was completely misunderstood, ridiculed and mistrusted in the beginning. Now it is more than acceptable; it is a widespread, respected, "conventional" and certainly very profitable way of doing business.

Network Marketing is a business idea that is not understood by most people, yet it is the most advanced business concept available on the planet today—and it is so simple that anyone can learn to become very successful in a short time.

After reading this book, you may decide that this is the door you've been searching for.

Make a decision to check out an alternative financial vehicle. Successful people check out opportunities, and most wealthy people have more than one source of income. They are diversified, and you will probably want to consider doing the same thing.

Diversify your income now—while you can.

Why wait until something happens to your job?

Why wait until something happens to you and you can't work?

Why wait until you retire?

You can start right now.

By following the success system in this book, you will have the option of retiring early from your present job or other business, if you choose. You will be able to chart your own course in life. You can be financially free in only two to five years.

My two college degrees are in business: one in marketing, the other in real estate. Looking back, I see that our educational system is geared for placing people in jobs, teaching them how to work for someone else. A Master of Business Administration (MBA) degree is really a degree in how to run *someone else's* business.

This educational practice is left over from the Industrial Revolution, when factories needed people to show up and do what they were told. In business school, I was never taught how to start and run a business—not one course, not one lecture. I was not taught how to organize people to create sales volume in the marketplace—the source of all wealth and income in the world.

I was taught to work for someone else.

Professor Jack Tenge, Ph.D., made a permanent, positive impression on me. He was talking about getting a job, but his lecture could have been applied to starting a business. He said to remember three things:

- One: Look for opportunity, not a high paying position. Today's opportunity will be tomorrow's high paying business. Today's high paying business was yesterday's opportunity.

- Two: Find your opportunity and build your future in consumer products and services. The consumer market is where you can create large, dependable sales volume and stability with products and services that people will always need and buy.

- Three: Find an existing company or product that is misunderstood or not understood, and then reposition people's minds; help them to change the way they think about the product or the company, so they can start enjoying the benefits it offers.

This book is about a business idea that is today's foremost opportunity in consumer products and services—an idea that is misunderstood and not understood, and yet many people are becoming very successful with it.
You can become very successful with it, too.

It has been said that there are three kinds of people:

1) Those who make things happen;
2) Those who watch or let things happen;
3) Those who don't know what's happening.

You determine your own future.
You are responsible for creating your own life.
If you do not believe that, then you are faced with the alternative of blaming people and circumstances for your own failings. Remember, it's not what happens to you that matters; it's what you do about it that matters.
Take charge.

Do you think of yourself as the President of your own Personal Services Corporation? You are. You are already self-employed, because you sell your time to the highest bidder in the marketplace (your present employer).
You're always free to negotiate with another buyer who will pay you more for your time. You're already in business for yourself and you always have been. You've been selling your time on the open market since the first day you went to work.

To be successful, you may need to change the way you think about prestige and status. You'll have to ignore the people and the advertising that try to make you think you need to act in certain ways, that you need to buy certain things, expensive things, in order to count for something.

It's a lie.

I used to suffer from status. I had it real bad. But I got over it as I grew older and realized status wasn't going to pay any of my bills.

A poll by J. Walter Thompson Advertising found that careers with the highest status pay the least: fireman, paramedic, farmer, pharmacist, grade school teacher, mail carrier, priest, housekeeper, baby sitter, college professor.

You know what's interesting?

The occupations considered the sleaziest were the most lucrative: drug dealer, crime boss, prostitute, street peddler, local politician, congressman, car salesman, rock and roll star, insurance salesman.

Prestige and high income do not go together. Never have. Two of the largest, wealth creating industries in the world are the distribution of oil and the distribution of household products, and neither one has any status at all.

It's your choice.

You can try to "look good" and stay broke, or you can become wealthy and free by providing legal, necessary consumer products and services to an unlimited number of people through your own independent business that leverages your time to the highest degree possible.

Decide right now that you don't care what other people think.

They aren't thinking about you anyway. They're thinking about themselves, worrying about their own problems and wondering what you think about them.

And *they* don't pay your bills, either.

After you read this book you'll have enough information to make the decision to become rich and free in the next two to five years, to become part of the five percent of Americans who are financially independent and excited about life at age 65 and beyond.

And you'll learn how to become part of the *one percent* group who earn increasing six-figure incomes every year. You'll learn how to create a six-figure income for the rest of your life!

When I was first exposed to the information and the ideas in this book, I felt a glimmer of hope flicker in my heart. I sure hoped it was true. I wanted a better way to live, and I knew there was more to life than I had experienced so far.

Now I know, if just one person can do it, then you can learn to do it, too.

This business idea is not new; Network Marketing has been a successful business concept since the 1940s. But now it is suddenly becoming a very popular way of doing business. And that's because it is more effective and more efficient than any "business as usual," and it's a powerful way to create residual income. For most people, it's the *only* way!

You can become anything you want to be, and you can do anything you want to do. All that is required is that you become a student of a unique way of doing business and follow a proven success system for building your own Network Marketing business.

Learn to own your future.

Learn to leverage time.

Learn an exciting way to organize people for mutual benefit, and help them to become successful, too.

Learn to follow the people who are where you want to be.

Learn to do the same things they did to get there.

Turn the page and learn . . . .

CHAPTER 2
The Three Ways to Make Money

There are a million ways to make a buck, says the proverbial wisdom. Just look at all the employment offers in the classified advertisements. You'll find all kinds of ways to make money. Go ask a career counselor. You'll be overwhelmed with the choices available for making a living.

But you know what? They are really all the same. They are all jobs.

There are only three ways to make money.

1) Trade your time for dollars.
2) Invest your money to earn more money.
3) Invest your time to create both more time and more money.

Let's look at each of the three.

Way One: Trading Your Time For Money

All of those employment descriptions in the help-wanted ads are jobs. They are examples of the first way of making money—trading your time for dollars. You show up, you put in your time, you get paid. And, you hope it lasts.

All employees and all self-employed people fall into this first category. If you have to be there to get paid—it's a job.

A job is a financial leash. It limits how far you can go. It tethers your future. At best, it might pay you about 25 percent of what you are really worth—probably less. Look, your employer has to make money—right? The way to do that is to pay you less than he or she charges customers for what you produce.

People using this financial vehicle never have any time to do anything else, because they spend it all chasing money. For people with a job, time is money—literally. When you don't put in the time, you don't get any money. So, you work all the time, trying to get ahead, hoping that working longer and working harder will bring success.

Remember the fly?

You know that doesn't work.

No matter how hard you work, it doesn't seem to matter. Working harder and working more hours is not the answer. You're on a treadmill, and it's deadly stressful.

Tell me, if you worked twice as long—would you earn twice as much?

If you worked twice as hard—would you earn twice the income?

Could you work twice as hard or twice as many hours as you do now?

It's a dead end!

Self-employed people face the same challenge. It is a job if you have to be there. It's a job if your income is limited by the amount of time that you can spend working. This is true for highly paid doctors and lawyers, too. If they don't show up, they don't get paid.

Depending on a job—even a big job—for your security is like committing financial suicide. And besides, life is too short for a full-time job.

Depending on a job for your identity is like murdering your self-image. You are not your job, and status doesn't pay very well. Especially if you're its prisoner.

Is this crazy talk?

That depends on whether or not you're looking for a way out of the economic rut that keeps you broke and frustrated. It's not crazy to want to escape the thunderous stampede of the mindless majority. Figure out which way everyone else is going—then go the other way! Follow your own leader— follow yourself! And you start by being open to exploring other ways of making money.

There is no such thing as job security, not anymore. It isn't even *your* job. You don't own it. The term itself, "job security," is an oxymoron—the two words contradict each other.

Neither education nor seniority can guarantee your security in a job. That's a myth. It's often said that J.O.B. is an acronym for Just Over Broke, which is where your job will keep you. Your job holds you hostage.

Forget the gold watch. Lifetime employment is obsolete. You are not likely to stay with any company long enough to reach retirement anymore.

These days, most people will change jobs as many as seven times before they retire—and that's *seven different companies,* not just promotions. Seven different layoffs. Seven different job searches.

This first way of making money was not designed for your success. It's for your employer. It yokes you to a spoke on a wheel, and you walk in circles in a rut, turning the gears for someone else's success. Just because you walked all day doesn't mean you got anywhere.

Less than one percent of the millionaires in America made their fortunes by trading time for money at a job. Yet, 95 percent of Americans are using this one financial vehicle to make a living and to try to accomplish their goals—if they have any left.

If the majority were right, they'd be rich. But the majority of people are broke.

This is called the rut system by people who got out of it and discovered a better financial vehicle.

I call a job the 40-40-40 plan. You put in 40 hours a week for 40 years, and they're supposed to take care of you and make sure you have a nice retirement with your $40 watch.

Just look at these statistics:

- More than half of all executives regularly work not 40, but more than 59 hours a week.

- 50 percent of all retirees enter retirement with less than $10,000 in savings and can look forward to living on one third to one half of their former salary.

- The average 50-year-old has accumulated only $2,300 in savings and investments, not counting a home. If you are that average 50-year-old, your summer vacation will wipe out your life savings.

- The "average person" is carrying $15,000 in consumer debt, not counting mortgages and cars, and that makes it impossible to save for retirement.

If you are under 35, you may never see a Social Security check. It might be Social Insecurity for you.

Originally, the Social Security Administration said there would be 30 workers paying into the system to support every retiree. (Isn't that a beautiful pyramid scheme?) In 1955, the ratio had fallen to six workers for every retiree. Today it is three workers for every retiree. That's the trouble with pyramid schemes. The last ones in lose!

And right now, you're one of the last ones.

The baby-boom generation with its buy-now-pay-later attitude is entering their "pre-retirement" period, those 20 years prior to hitting age 65. Very few people, especially baby-boomers, will save enough money to support themselves in retirement. It is going to be a rude awakening for them. The longer they wait to save money for retirement, the deeper the hole they dig for themselves.

According to Social Security, if you are 40 years old and you're now earning $40,000 a year, when you retire at age 66, your retirement benefits will amount to $1,183 per month. That's $14,000 a year. 35 percent of your pre-retirement income.

Good luck!

Do you know how much you'll need to start saving—right now—to have a retirement income of say $25,000 annually? You'll need a total of $450,000 to live off the interest. If I started you off with $8,000 in the bank—today—all you'd have to save every month from now on would be $900 each month tax-deferred.

No wonder people are desperate!

More companies are telling their employees to start planning for their own retirement. With rising medical costs and shrinking job tenure, employers are shifting the investment risk to employees; they are switching from defined-benefit to defined-contribution plans.

Many workers will not have sufficient pension benefits to support retirement. Saving more and earlier and investing savings more aggressively are the keys to protecting your own retirement.

People carry around this myth that somehow they are going to be okay. But they aren't even close to being okay. They wake up at 40 and they freak!

To retire, you are going to need at least 75 percent of what you earned (after taxes and savings) during your working days. Your pensions and Social Security income will probably provide you with only 30 percent to 50 percent of your former salary—at best! Your expenses for commuting and dry cleaning will go down, but travel and medical costs might rise.

Most people settle for less in retirement. They cut back on their expectations. Why do that? Is that what you want? Is that what you worked your whole life for? Why not travel the world and do all the things you have dreamed of doing all your life?

You'll need at least 100 percent of your former income if you have plans for an exciting retirement.

What are you going to do?

Let's say, for example, that you are now 40 years of age and earning $120,000 a year.

How much of that are you saving?

If you are saving less than $25,000, you are headed for retirement trouble. Saving is tough. You'll have to get by on $60,000 a year, after taxes. That's a bitter pill. And it gets worse.

Adjusting for estimated inflation and increasing taxes, and assuming your $120,000 income merely keeps up with the cost of living, you will need $80,000 in income to maintain your standard of living in retirement at 65.

Optimistically, assume your Social Security check will be there for you and contributes $10,000 a year, and let's hope you were able to develop a pension plan as well, that delivers another $20,000. That's only $30,000, and you are $50,000 short. The difference has to come from the income on your savings, interest or dividends. You will need a savings pot of *$1.25 million* earning four percent to provide the $50,000 that you will need. Yet, assuming an inflation rate of four percent, the actual yield on your investments will need to be at least eight percent.

Only 24 percent of all Americans believe their retirement finances will enable them to live comfortably.

14 percent expect not to have enough to live on.

29 percent do not know what their retirement incomes will be.

71 percent worry that their medical expenses will outdistance their income.

60 percent worry about outliving their retirement income.

49 percent worry about becoming disabled.

And we call retirement the "Golden Years"?

Take 100 workers at retirement, as the Hartford Insurance company did in 1992:

One is wealthy.

Four are financially independent.

16 are still working

80 are broke and dependent on family and the government—or else they didn't make it to 65, because of the deadly stress and financial pressures of worrying about making a living.

That means that 90 percent of Americans at age 65 are either dead, broke, or still working. They did not plan to fail, they failed to plan. In the richest nation in the world, only five percent of the population realizes financial independence by age 65.

But why retire—and suffer—when you can create a residual, six-figure income that will last a lifetime? Why not start a business that will take care of you all the way to the end—and then take care of your loved ones for years after you're gone?

Why depend on someone else?

Why limit your—and your family's future?

Why gamble with *that?*

A job takes your time and gives you money—not a living, just money, and less than you deserve—in return. Your productive time is your only real asset. Spending your time, selling your time for a paycheck, you continually face the challenge of truly making a living.

Your time is a limited, non-renewable resource. You have only 24 hours a day, 168 hours a week. And that's the same amount as everyone else has, too. So, you do have time, but it's limited; and when it's gone, it's gone for good.

Having time is a matter of ordering the priorities in your life. When you know what's important, you make the time for it—don't you?

When you know where you want to go, you'll make the time to do what it takes to get there. It's your choice; you can stay broke with a job and be a P.O.W. (prisoner of work), just making a living . . . . or you can step up to a highly developed financial vehicle and start *making a life.*

With a job, you can chart your productive life on the following graph (see Diagram 1):

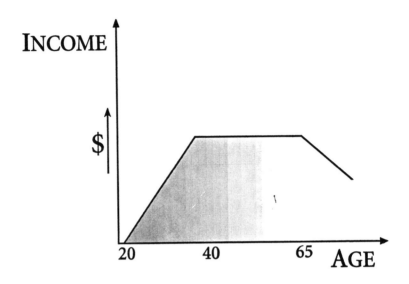

Diagram 1: Income Graph

Most people start their serious working lives at around age 20. Their income shoots up dramatically until around the age of 40, and after that it plateaus until age 65 when, for most people, it falls off to one half to one third of what they had been earning previously.

Most people at age 25 take for granted that they will be fabulously successful—some day. They know that some day they will get all the things they want, and will do everything they dream of doing.

Then they reach age 35 and realize they better get serious.

They hit the so-called "mid-life" 40s and they give up. Their incomes level out. Their careers plateau.

They start to shrink their expectations.

They start to doubt if they'll really accomplish everything they set out to do.

They hide in front of the television after dinner and on weekends instead of getting out of the house and doing something to secure their future.

They adjust their goals to their income—instead of the other way around.

In the past, the only two ways to break through the income plateau were to make your time more valuable with more education, or with more experience—or both.

Many people have found out that advanced university degrees do not guarantee security or higher earnings today. That's the myth of education.

I'm all for education. Life should be a continuing educational process that does not stop when formal education stops.

But today there is no correlation between college degrees and steadily increasing earnings. There is no connection between higher education and financial security.

In order to charge more for your experience, you may have to change employers, and switching jobs is a big challenge. It's always difficult to find a new job that pays more than the last one, simply on the basis of your vast experience.

The thing is, even if you do get a better paying position, because of your higher education and experience, your income will eventually top out again. You'll plateau at a higher level, that's all—and you'll probably have higher income and higher debt, too. Your lifestyle and expenses will always rise to meet (or exceed) your income when you have a job.

A job is not the best financial vehicle for creating the life and the security that you want. Trading time for dollars constricts your future.

The following graph (see Diagram 2) shows what can happen with a different kind of financial vehicle, one where your income keeps increasing indefinitely.

If you had this kind of income, would you worry about retirement?

Would you even consider retirement?

No. You would be too excited about life and your future.

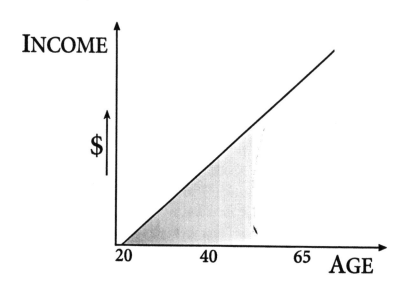

Diagram 2: Income Graph

Many people—perhaps even some people you know right now—already have this kind of unlimited income, and their lives just keep getting better and more exciting.

They do not consider cutting back and living on less.

They have grandiose plans for their lives, and they know they will have the income to dream and plan as big as they want.

They travel.

They live in dream homes.

They support all kinds of charities and community services.

They don't worry about money.

They are relaxed.

They are free.

They look and feel younger.

How would you live if you did not have to worry about money?

How would you live if you were not controlled by time?

You can look forward to enjoying residual income also, and the surprising thing is that it is available for you in the next two to five years, and it can keep getting bigger and better. Forget the 40-40-40 approach to life. Take the two to five year plan instead.

It doesn't matter how young or old you are.

It doesn't matter how much education you have or how much experience you have.

It doesn't matter how deep your current rut is.

You can open your mind and learn to use a different financial vehicle.

You can start right now right where you are.

You do not need to do anything else first.

You can change your habits and your attitudes.

You can earn while you learn.

You can!

Way Two: Investing Your Money

The second way of making money is to leverage your savings or other money that you've either borrowed or don't need to live on. You can invest that money in the stock market, real estate, limited partnerships, mutual funds, or other investment vehicles.

An investment is not the same as your savings. Of course, you need to save money, too, but the bank savings accounts, Certificates of Deposit (CDs), Treasury Bills (T-Bills) and other money market accounts do not actually pay enough interest to really qualify as money-making investments. These are simply safe places for keeping your cash. But the minimum interest rates of these "investments" guarantee that you will lose money, because taxes and inflation will eat up whatever interest you earn.

Let's say your one dollar in a savings account earns four percent interest. Remember, that is *taxable* income. And let's say you are in the highest tax bracket, paying nearly 50 percent in state and federal income taxes. That means you are two percent ahead.

Inflation is around four percent. So, you are actually losing two per-cent—$2 on every $100—every year. The only advantage here is that your money is available to you right away if you need it. And it is relatively safe.

But when you leverage your money in investments, you create more money—at least potentially. Now, your money is working *for* you. 14 per-cent of the millionaires in America created their fortunes this way. Yet only two percent of us regular people create our principal incomes this way.

All investments carry some risk. You might lose your money, and most people do. The percentage of investors who continually profit from their investments is low. More likely, you lose on one and then win on the next one, and your investment record is a roller coaster of profits and losses. So you must be able to afford to lose to play the game at all.

The real barrier to investing for most people is that you must have the extra money in the first place.

Few people ever have enough money to invest such that they create a consistent and dependable investment income. Also, you need specialized skills, knowledge and experience to analyze and manage your investment opportunities.

Never rely totally on someone else to invest your money. Their reasons are different from your reasons for buying the investment. You may be look-ing for long-term safety and enduring performance. But they're looking at the short-term commission.

Do you know who really makes money from investments?

Brokers.

Way Three: Investing Your Time

The third way of making money is to leverage, or invest, your time in other people. Leveraging time is the real key to all lasting wealth in America. When you leverage your time, you create more time and more money. 85 percent of the millionaires in America created their fortunes this way—yet only three percent of us are doing this.

Why?

The key to wealth and freedom is people. Look at this—a word of advice from one of history's richest men, J. Paul Getty:

"I would rather earn one percent of a hundred people's efforts than 100 percent of my own."

You must learn to organize other people for mutual benefit with an attractive financial vehicle.

When you help enough other people to get what they want in life, then you can have whatever you want. You need to own a business vehicle that leverages time.

In America, and in more and more of the world every day, the name of the money (and power) game is business.

And in business, the name of the game is sales volume.

In volume lies profit. Every business strives to serve the greatest possible number of people and to create the greatest possible volume of products and services sold with the least amount of expenses. The purpose of a business is to create and keep a customer, and in that process to create an increasing volume of products and services.

The American Dream of personal freedom and financial independence is available to anyone who can gain control of this consumer volume.

The marketplace pays only for sales volume. The actual product or service hardly matters at all. It doesn't matter whether you move computers or kitchen cabinets. Lawyers and chefs both create sales volume. Every single job contributes to sales volume, however insignificant—or it is eliminated.

We all serve people in the process of moving products and services. More sales volume equals more income. The important things are the potential demand and the capability of the distribution system for the products or services that you move. The main thing is serving an unlimited number of people.

When you control the volume, you control your future.

With the exceptions of marrying money or winning money or finding money, you will become truly wealthy *only* as a result of doing one of the following:

1) By owning a business that lets you leverage time and control sales volume;

2) By inheriting a fortune and managing it well (i.e., keeping it);

3) By investing very wisely and fortuitously all your life.

True wealth always includes these four factors:

A) Cash flow

B) Net worth on paper from investments

C) Favorable income tax position

D) Discretionary time

I've written again and again that time is the key. Let's look now at ways you can leverage your time.

CHAPTER 3
The Four Ways to Leverage Time

Nobody makes it big all alone. If they seem to, don't worry. It won't last long. You need the help, energy, efforts and creative ideas of a team of people to build a substantial business with reliable income and growth—and growth requires leverage.

The history of business is the chronicle of people finding better ways to leverage time. All business owners want residual income—money that keeps coming in even when they are not there physically working, running the business.

All businesses are organized with the intent of creating residual income for the owners. Most businesses are seriously flawed in this regard, and their potential for creating unlimited income is constrained by many factors.

Entrepreneurs have always found creative ways to organize people that continue to produce sales volume and income, even when the business owner was not physically present. The history of business is the story of the pursuit of residual income, and that's why it is also the history of leveraging time.

The beginning of free enterprise in America was the self-sufficient farmer bartering with his neighbor. If you were good at making candles and your neighbor made excellent jam, you would trade with each other.

Soon, money became more valuable, because you could use it buy things from people who didn't want your candles. So, you sold your candles for cash instead of trading them.

You were in the candle business.

You found out very quickly that you could make only so many candles in a day.

You realized the limits of your own time and effort.

Your income from your candle business peaked.

But that wasn't so bad. You had a successful candle business, even though it was not growing. You were serving people by providing products they needed. You had created a certain amount of sales volume. You didn't have any competition. Most of your neighbors and family thought you were doing very well.

The problem was that you were ambitious and wanted more income, but your business had no leverage. The question was how to increase the number of candles you could make in a day, since you had to stop to eat and sleep, and you were already working as many hours as it was possible to work.

You had no more time to put into the business.

You needed a better way to serve more people and create more volume.

Picture one lone, tired circle: that's your business. It's just you, your supplier and some customers.

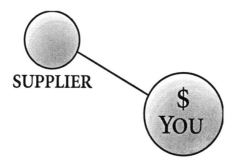

Diagram 3: Individual and Supplier

You have total responsibility for all decisions and income. It's a job; you have to be there or you don't get paid.

You are trading your hours for dollars.

You work all the time.

You plow your profits back into the business to stimulate growth, so you aren't personally enjoying the results of your success yet.

It is a treadmill, and you cannot get off or slow down.

One solution is to bring in a partner, but a partner will want to own part of the business. You don't want to give away part of the business that you have built with your own sweat, courage and all those sleepless nights. You don't want to give up any creative control. You don't want to share the responsibility or the profits.

Solution: You need to leverage your time.

There are four ways to leverage time in a business.

One: Hire Employees

Hiring employees creates minimal leverage. You can serve more people and create more sales volume in your business when you have people to help you do it.

Picture your lone, weary circle and draw one or more circles beneath it, connected by short lines of control. These circles are your employees.

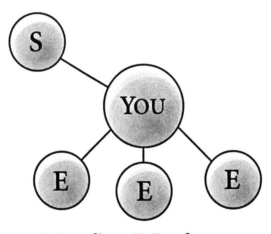

S: Supplier   E: Employees

Diagram 4: Individual, Supplier and Employees

By hiring employees, you can somewhat duplicate your time and effort. Employees do not require ownership in the business, and you usually only need to pay them less than 25 percent of their actual productivity and contribution to your business volume.

The Limitations Of Hiring Employees

When you start a business that relies on employees for creating sales volume, then, in order to grow, you will always need more employees.

In the early 1990s, we watched the huge landmarks of the American business landscape shed employees the way a giant oak tree sheds its leaves in the fall. Sears, IBM, Kodak, General Motors, Hewlett-Packard, AT&T, and many, many others realized they didn't need and could not afford so many employees. Medium-sized companies followed the same route, and the small firms will eliminate unnecessary jobs, too. It is a process experts say will last through the 1990s. Unfortunately, those jobs are not going to grow back in the "spring" of economic recovery.

Often, employees are interested in doing very little in return for their paychecks, and they are notoriously unreliable and expensive. Some of them are downright hard to get along with. Theft and absenteeism are expensive problems that often come with employees.

This is a generalization, of course. The really good employees work hard and learn as much as they can about the business. They become very good managers of your business. But then, one day, they become your competitor when they quit, opening their own business right across the street from you.

Employees are, however, an unavoidable fact of life in running a conventional business.

The myth of business as usual is the idea that you can build up your business volume and your customers, and then you get a good manager to run your business for you while you sit back and take it easy and enjoy the fruits of your labor. It never happens.

While the cat is away the mice do play. Nobody will run your business and take care of your customers the way you do. You are the magic that built the business, and if you are not there, the business will vaporize.

Unfortunately, the number of employees that you can hire is limited. You have only a certain amount of space, and they take up room. They need desks and equipment and telephones and tools. You can fit only so many of them in your shop.

They cost money.

They have to be paid regularly, and they ask for raises.

They demand all kinds of benefits like health insurance and vacation pay, and the government makes you pay part of their taxes.

So, the bottom line is that even if you have the physical space for more of them, you probably can't afford to hire more.

If you had more sales volume you could afford more employees, but you need more employees to create more sales volume. It's a catch 22.

Your business must keep growing. This is an indisputable law of the nature of commerce. Either your business grows or it dies.

Long-term, there is no middle ground. If the business sits still, complacency on the inside or competitors on the outside will destroy it. Growth is required, but growth requires capital.

So, your business has plateaued again. You're back where you started when it was only you—except now, all the numbers are larger. Your income is bigger but your expenses are bigger, too. You are topped out and tapped out.

Same bottom-line problem as before, but this time it's different.

You see no easy way to expand.

You have no room to grow in your current location.

Competition in the marketplace prevents you from moving your business to larger quarters, and besides, the main reason for your success is your excellent, present location.

What's your next step for continued growth and survival?

Create width.

Two: Expand With Chain Stores

You discover a growing area across town. It presents an opportunity for you to open a second business identical to your first one. So, you duplicate your successful operation. Now you have two locations. Sears and J.C. Penny and other chain store operations started this way. So can you.

Or can you . . . ?

This growth is known as horizontal leverage, or width.

Picture your business with your circles of employees below, and draw an identical structure beside it, and put a manager in it, too.

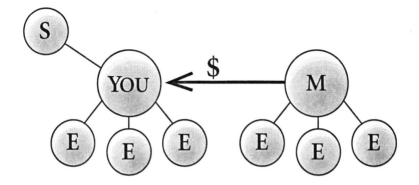

S: Supplier   M: Manager   E: Employees

Diagram 5: Individual with two stores

Now, all you need to do is be in two places at once. You concentrate on training your employees, so they will run the business the way you want it to be run while you are working at the second location.

Your sales volume and profits climb steadily.

You are purchasing larger orders of supplies and enjoying volume discounts from your suppliers.

You are serving more people and creating more volume.

You are more profitable than before.

And . . . you have less time than ever.

Suddenly you have the opportunity to open three more locations in nearby towns. You borrow the money from the bank for your expansion.

Draw three circles just like the first two, all side by side.

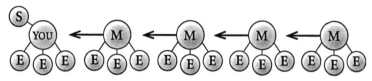

S: Supplier   M: Manager   E: Employees

Diagram 6: Individual owning chain of stores

Now you are really handling the money.

You control an army of employees.

You have trained some reliable managers, for now.

You know that you are on your way to becoming wealthy!

However, you have too much debt from borrowing the money to open the three new locations. Costs have risen for everything you buy. Your business is not turning the profits as fast as you had anticipated. The economy has slowed. Competitors are turning up the heat.

Business is okay, but you are topped out again, this time with a staggering cash flow, incredible expenses, monumental debt load, a huge employee responsibility, and a ton of financial and regulatory problems.

Your business seems to be hugely successful, but no one realizes the scope of the financial pressure that you live with—and you would do anything to get control of your time.

You have sacrificed other areas of your life, like family, recreation and personal pursuits, to reach this point in the business.

Your success is unbalanced.

You wonder if it is worth it.

You want your time back—*please!*

The Limitations Of Opening Chain Stores

You know the business must continue its growth if it is to survive. You cannot open any more locations, because you don't have the money and you can't borrow any more. You have created a monster of a job for yourself.

And isn't that interesting . . . ?

You started out owning your own business, and now, what you own is your own job. And a monster one at that!

The second way of leveraging time, opening chain stores, is in reality a vastly more complicated variation of hiring more employees.

Opening more locations creates only width—no depth. Width takes all your time. You own the business, but it seems like the business owns and controls you now.

Owning or leasing more real estate and setting up businesses with all the necessary equipment, inventory and employees is prohibitively expensive. Along with the unceasing job cutbacks of the 90s, we are witnessing a serious trend in cutting back on commercial real estate, too.

But you are committed to building the business, so selling out is not an option.

What's your next step for continued growth?

Create depth.

Three: Franchise Your Business

The third way of leveraging time, franchising, was a magic answer to all the problems created by the need for more employees and commercial space. The main reasons franchising has been such a phenomenal success are that it does not rely on employees for growth, and it creates one level of depth that produces greater sales volume and residual income for the franchisor.

Few people understood franchising prior to the 1970s. In fact, most people were afraid of the idea. They thought a franchise was a pyramid scheme. In fact, the first big franchise operations did not use the word "franchise" in their business opportunity advertising because of its negative connotations.

Today, we are surrounded by successful franchises. Franchising is one of the most widely accepted and profitable ways of building a business. Every freeway off ramp is crowded with franchises: fast foods, convenience stores, motels, and others.

Some of the very first franchises were churches (think about that!) and gasoline stations. McDonalds and Kentucky Fried Chicken are among the famous success stories in the franchising industry.

Now, with franchises in hand, let's return to your business dilemma. You were topped out with five locations. Your income and your opportunities for growth had plateaued, once again. You knew there were untapped opportunities to open more locations and to create more volume by serving more people, but you did not have the resources to open them. Yet, you imagined your business operating successfully on a national scale.

Your next step is to sell other people the right to duplicate your business success.

So . . .

You find some people who want to own their own businesses.

You charge them a small fortune for your proven business plan and for your expertise, which you promise to teach them, and for the advertising that you promise to run to help them succeed.

Picture your own five businesses, side by side—your business width. Now, draw as many duplicates of your businesses as you can fit on the page, side by side below your business.

This is your business depth.

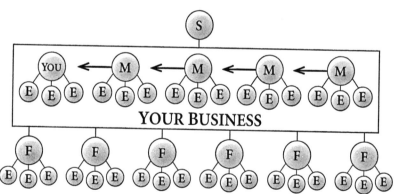

S: Supplier   M: Manager   F: Franchisee   E: Employees

Diagram 7: Individual with several franchises

It wasn't easy, but now you've found qualified people with experience, money and ambition and you've sold many franchisees.

You help set them start up in business and teach them to duplicate your proven operation.

You offer ongoing training, and you make sure they duplicate everything that you did to succeed in your business. When they duplicate your system, they duplicate both the success and the profits.

You have an ongoing interest in their success, because you share in their success. They pay you a percentage of their sales. When they make money, you both make money.

Also, you don't make any money unless they do. That's residual income to you. They buy supplies from you, which is profitable and which gives you greater volume discounts which contribute to the profits of your own locations.

You become wealthy selling franchises; but eventually, after a number of years, your business volume is topped out again. The growth of your business slows, because you have exhausted all of the most desirable locations across the entire country. Your franchised business name is on successful businesses on freeway intersections and in malls throughout the country.

Competition is intense.

The economy is weak.

Profit margins are thin.

You've been here before.

Your business volume has plateaued once again.

Now you are very rich, and you have created the American Dream—but somehow, money doesn't matter anymore.

You have more money than you will ever need.

You sold your five original locations to the managers who are now franchisees.

You have your time back.

Your motivation for working is based on the challenge of building the business, not because you need the money.

You are sincerely interested in helping other people succeed.

Now the business is huge, but it has plateaued.

What's next? International expansion: Russia. The Pacific Rim. Latin America. There are over a hundred countries world-wide that welcome American business expansion.

However, you don't know anything about foreign business.

You know it is expensive and risky.

You are not willing to commit your time and resources to such an uncertain, risky move.

It's at this point in the evolution of a successful business that many business owners sell out. They hit the wall in terms of further development and growth. But when they stop growing, they risk stagnation.

The Limitations of Franchising

The problem with business as usual is that your sales volume and your income always plateau at a higher level, and it takes more resources to sustain further growth.

Franchising is only a golden opportunity for the business owner who is selling the franchise opportunity. For the entrepreneur who buys a franchise, it is just business as usual, with all of the limitations and headaches of running a small, conventional business with employees. His or her chances of success are greater than the entrepreneur striking out alone, because there is a proven system to follow, but that's about the only benefit of buying a franchise.

They are still trading time for dollars, because they have to be there to create the volume. They are just buying and owning a job—a job more complex and stressful then any other job imaginable!

The person who starts a business by buying a franchise opportunity cannot expand the business when the volume and the profits plateau. She can't open another location on her own, and she can't sell a franchise opportunity.

The only way to grow is to buy another franchise. Since franchises have protected territories, there may not be one available in her area. If one is available, she may not have the many thousands of dollars (remember, the average fee is $85,000—and that's only the fee itself!) required to buy it.

Franchising creates one level of depth, which produces residual income, and that feature made it far superior to chain stores with employees, but . . .

The main limitations of franchising are:

1) The person who buys a franchise cannot expand the business, and . . .

2) Not everyone can get involved, because of various qualifications required, such as previous experience in business, a credit history, and having the money to buy and keep one operating.

Four: Network Marketing

Network Marketing, the fourth way of leveraging time, is an exciting, effective business idea that solves the limitations of franchising. It goes one step further in the quest for creating residual income. It adds *unlimited business depth.*

Network Marketing is a business concept that has been misunderstood and mistrusted in the same way that franchising was not accepted in its early days in the 60s. The media and traditional business owners hear about Network Marketing; they think they see a pyramid scheme—and they run away in fear.

So, just what is a pyramid?

The government is a pyramid: look at all the layers of employees, wider and wider as you go down, that it takes to run the business of collecting taxes and administering services.

General Motors and IBM are pyramids. The stockholders and board of directors select a company president to put at the top of the pyramid. Under the president is a layer of officers, another layer of executives, another layer of managers, and layers and layers *and layers* of employees, wider and wider as you go down.

All businesses, churches, and local and national governments organize people in the form of pyramids.

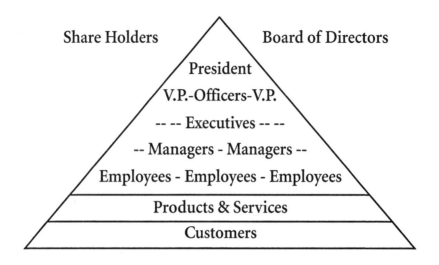

Diagram 8: Corporate pyramid

An illegal pyramid is a fraud where people give their money to a so-called business owner who doesn't give them anything of value in return. Perhaps he teaches them how to rip off their friends, promising that they'll all get a lot more money later, but *they* all get ripped off instead.

Pyramid schemes that defraud people are illegal and should be condemned.

Social Security is the only "legal" pyramid scheme I know of.

Network Marketing is a unique business idea. It is not an illegal pyramid scheme.

It has all the advantages of the other three ways of leveraging time in a business, but none of their limitations.

Network Marketing adds an unlimited vertical dimension of depth that is made possible with today's computers. It is "in-depth marketing."

In "business as usual," depth is called "referral business" or "word of mouth" business, but it cannot be reliably re-created or repeated. It happens by accident.

In Network Marketing, anybody at any level in the business can expand the business Network because there are no territorial restrictions. Anyone can get involved in a Network Marketing business opportunity, because it requires very little money, very little time, and no other mandatory qualifications to get started.

Just as with a franchise, with a Network Marketing business you have a supplier and a support system with a training program and a proven system to follow.

But unlike the situation with a franchisee, when your business volume tops out, you can continue to grow by bringing business associates—not employees, but *independent contractors* like yourself who own their own businesses—into your Network, just as if you were selling your own mini-franchises. And they, in turn, can do the same thing, and on, and on.

Where franchising creates limited width and only one level of depth, Network Marketing creates unlimited width and unlimited depth—and what's more, it creates the potential for unlimited sales volume!

Picture yourself with one small marketing business (and I do mean *small:* a typical Network Marketer may have only a handful of regular retail clients). You have a reliable supplier for quality, competitive products and services that people need and want to buy.

You have a support system for training and motivation.

You have a few good customers.

You have no employees, no overhead, no capital requirements, and no debt.

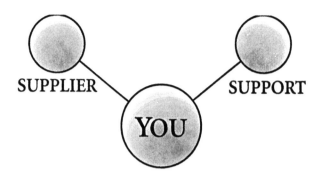

Diagram 9: A Simple Network

You are the business.

You receive performance bonuses and wholesale/retail rebates based primarily on the small amount of products and services that you consume personally in your household.

Your retail sales to customers are minimal.

You are ambitious, and you want to create more volume.

Your business has to grow in order to survive and prosper.

In Network Marketing, you can sponsor new businesses in much the same way that you sold franchises.

Think big.

Teach them how to be successful, knowing that when they duplicate a successful system, they will duplicate the profits, too.

Supply them with training, promotional materials, products and services to get them started in the business correctly.

Picture a layer of identical businesses associates—not employees—right beside yours, spread out in width, as many as you want.

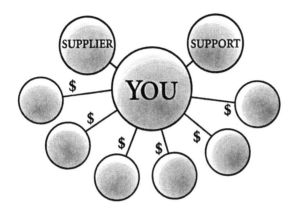

Diagram 10: Intermediate Network

The business associates whom you sponsored are ambitious, like you, and they want to create large businesses that can create unlimited sales volume, also. They can sponsor new businesses into the Network and train and supply them, too.

You are interested in their growth because you earn residual income on the total volume of products and services sold through your business Network. So, you help them to explain the business to prospects, and you help to set up and train their new business owners.

Everyone has the same opportunity to grow and to become very successful. In fact, the people you sponsor have the opportunity to build a larger business than yours. The only criteria for success is the creation of sales volume. You get paid for your effort in direct proportion to your volume and sales results.

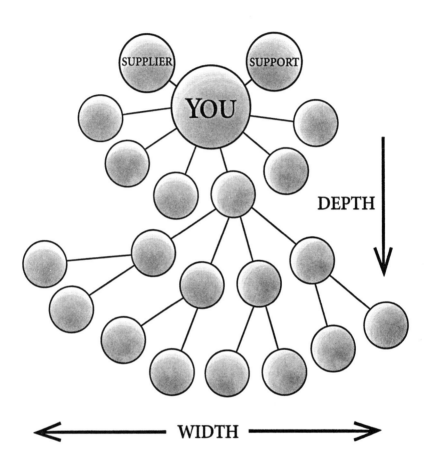

Diagram 11: Expanded Network

It is this element of unlimited depth that differentiates Network Marketing from franchising. Otherwise, it is a very similar structure. It is as
though Network Marketing has evolved directly out of the limitations of
franchising, just like franchising grew out of the limitations of retail chain
stores.

Computers make it possible to keep track of the volume in width and depth in the Network so that everyone in the Network earns a percentage, like a commission, for their share of the volume that they created in their Network.

Every business in the Network has a few retail customers and earns profits on the difference between the wholesale cost and retail price of the products and services they sell.

Every business earns residual income that is based on a percentage of the total volume created by all the other businesses in their Network.

Five percent of the volume comes from retail sales. 95 percent of the volume is residual income based on the total volume in the Network, which is primarily the result of purchases made by distributors for their personal use and their individual retail sales.

Network Marketing does not require employees.

Network Marketing does not require physical space.

Network Marketing does not require the capital and overhead needed to get started and to sustain continued growth, as in business as usual.

The opportunity to leverage time is unlimited in Network Marketing.

You can expand your width indefinitely since it costs you nothing but a small amount of your time invested in sponsoring and training new business associates.

You can expand your depth indefinitely, because everyone whom you bring into your business Network has the same opportunity that you have to build a business with unlimited width and depth. Every business in the Network is free to pursue the opportunity to leverage its time to the fullest with the intent of serving the greatest possible number of people and creating the largest possible sales volume of products and services.

Now, let's examine Network Marketing in detail in the next chapter.

CHAPTER 4
The Power of Network Marketing

Network Marketing is the most advanced concept in business today, yet it is such a simple idea. Network Marketing allows anyone to launch an independent business and immediately have access to a Network of products and/or services, all at wholesale discounts. It allows anyone to create a large, residual income on a flexible, part-time basis.

Network Marketing eliminates the middlemen and offers a profitable and personal business opportunity.

Network Marketing is an industry now approaching $100 billion a year world-wide, with millions and millions of people involved. 45,000 new people join Network Marketing every week around the world. The industry is growing at more than 20 percent a year. It is the fastest growing segment of the business economy today. Any business that can cut costs by eliminating unnecessary steps in distribution chain will be a successful business in the 90s and beyond.

Many interesting things are being said about Network Marketing today. Here's a sampling:

"Network Marketing is the wave of the future. People are interested in it, because it allows individuals to come together for a common cause. This enables them to get the attention of a manufacturer, an organization, or a service group. With this clout, they can meet their common goal."

—John Sestina, Certified Financial Planner

"The vertical to horizontal power shift that Networks bring about will be enormously liberating for individuals. Hierarchies promote moving up and getting ahead, producing stress, tension, and anxiety. Networking empowers the individual and people in the Networks to nurture one another."

—John Naisbitt, futurist and author

"A Network is the exact opposite of a bureaucracy. In a bureaucracy, the purpose is to collect power and distribute it down through a flow chart of underlings. In a Network, the purpose is to give power away. Many businesses are starting to Network. The essence of the recent trend, described in the fastest-selling business books, is to develop a win/win approach, to forget about your own quotas, to focus exclusively on how best to serve other people."

—Dr. Wayne Dyer, psychologist and author

"I was a salaried man. Now I am my own boss. Now I am free. Now I am helping people in five different countries to own their own businesses. When I see so many people getting more abundant lives, I feel really excited. This is no job to me. It is more like play."

—Kaoru Nakajima, Network Marketing distributor

"In most firms, work is a job. But in Network Marketing organizations, the company offers a mission and a way of life. Network Marketing revives the life-and-work style of the American frontier, when the family unit and economic unit were the same thing. Unlike a job, a Network Marketing business is founded explicitly on character and values and American free enterprise."

—Nicole Woolsey Biggart, UC Davis

"I used to think the only way to succeed was to climb the corporate ladder. But when I found out about Network Marketing I willingly gave up my six-figure income as a mortgage banker."
—Bill Hayden, Network Marketing distributor

"Visions of Wealth and Independence Lead Professionals to Try Multilevel [Network] Marketing."
—headline from *The Wall Street Journal*, June 23, 1995

"The more advanced the technology for delivery and home shopping, the more people need Network Marketing. It's carved out the essence, or the best part of retailing—educating people about products and services that will improve their lives and that they don't yet know exist—and that's what Network Marketing today is really all about."
—Paul Zane Pilzer, economist and author

"Network Marketing takes the frustration out of buying. People hate waiting in line. Nobody wants to go to stores anymore. As the person-to-person deliverers get classier, and better and more trusted, everything—from baskets to insurance—will be sold interactively, person-to-person . . . The retail environment is going to just have to close up. Nobody wants to go there. And Network Marketing has the solution."
—Faith Popcorn, futurist and author

"It is natural to cling to security. It's the type of security you are clinging to that makes the difference.

"Static security is clinging to a branch over a torrent of water, praying that the branch won't break. It's a kind of false security.

"Dynamic security is learning how to swim. Today, it's the only kind of security. And it's what Network Marketing offers."
—Scott DeGarmo, editor and publisher

"Network Marketing is the most powerful way to reach consumers in the 90s."
—Richard Poe, editor and author

How Do You Buy What You Buy?

Take a look for a moment at your own buying patterns. For example, where do you buy all of the conventional household products that you consume, all of the things that you buy and use every month, over and over?

Your home is full of consumer products. Mentally take inventory; check under your kitchen sink, in the pantry, in the laundry room, under the bathroom sink, in the shower, in the medicine cabinet, in the garage—your home is full of hundreds of products that you use day in and day out.

Here's another place to look: Do you, like millions of other Americans, have an interest in improving your health by using high quality nutritional products? A staggering number of the population at large are looking for answers to better health and well-being in places that only a decade ago would have been considered "alternative" or even "fringe."

And yet another: What about the services you routinely purchase—from from travel and financial instruments to entertainment and self-improvement?

Your household, like hundreds of millions of others, is a Grand Central Station of purchases and consumption, a constant, never-ending channel of products and services you will buy and use, again and again.

The question here is, how do you buy them?

The "A" System vs. the "B" System

There are two distribution systems that can provide you with all of the consumer products and services that you buy, use, and buy again, week after week, month after month. One system takes your money, the other pays you back.

The "A" System:
- The manufacturer produces products.
- The manufacturer sells to a jobber.
- The jobber sells to the wholesaler.
- The wholesaler sells to the retailer.
- The retailer sells to you, the customer.
- You use the product. That's it.

This is probably the system that has always supplied you with your consumer products and services. You are familiar with it—yes?

Maybe you're wondering, "What else is there?"

Indeed, your town is mainly made up of businesses that fit into this distribution system one way or another.

Let's say you are thinking of buying a coffee maker. The stores in your town sell it for a retail price of $100.

The manufacturer that makes the coffee maker charges the jobber $35 for it. That's 35 percent of the retail price, or a 65 percent discount. So, why don't you buy it from the manufacturer and save that money?

The "A" system won't let you. You would be cutting out the middleman—several of them. $65 of your $100 coffee maker goes to pay for all of the people in the "A" system to move that product along to the store where you can buy it. You are paying that "extra" money for truckers, shipping, warehousing, insurance, packing, advertising, promotion, merchandising, in addition to the wholesaler's and retailer's profits.

For some products, the cost of going through the "A" system is as high as 85 percent. That means when you pay a dollar for a box of cold cereal, you're probably getting only fifteen cents worth of actual cereal. The "A" system absorbs the rest of your money.

The "A" system includes the so-called wholesale outlets such as Costco, Price Club, Factory Stores, Sam's Club and many others. Interviews with Costco managers reveal that the overall savings at the "wholesale" warehouses are only seven to 10 percent—and further, you end up buying more than you need because of the bulk packaging.

The "B" System:
- Manufacturer
- Independent Distributor
- Customer

Network Marketing is the "B" system of distributing consumer products and services.

You don't see it.

Most people don't know about it.

The "B" system cuts out the middlemen so there are no warehouses or retail outlets.

When you get involved in the "B" system, you can become an independent distributor and purchase your products and services directly from the manufacturer at a real wholesale discount.

In the "B" system, the distributor is also the customer.

In this system, you can buy directly from the manufacturer. The savings will vary, but your wholesale discount will probably average 30 percent.

The "B" system also pays you a rebate on your total sales volume of products or services purchased by you or people in the Network you build. You can earn from three to 25 percent—with additional bonuses of up to 10 percent—all based on the sales volume that you create as an independent distributor. This is not to say that you exclusively go out and sell products to friends and neighbors; you can if you want to and you should, but that is not the whole idea.

When you buy the coffee maker from the "B" system, you might save 30 percent off the $100 retail price. You might also qualify for a rebate of up to 35 percent, depending on your total business volume. In other words, you could be getting the 65 percent that goes to the middleman in the "A" system.

The idea is to tell other people about the "B" system. Teach them how to take advantage of it to save money. When they purchase products and services through the Network, you earn a percentage, like a commission, of that sales volume.

Every distributor has a membership number, and the manufacturer has powerful computers to keep track of everyone's purchases, so you get credit for everything purchased by everyone whom you introduced to the Network and everyone they introduced to the Network, and so on.

I told my neighbor about this idea of leveraging time and making money.

She flatly rejected it. She didn't understand it. She wanted me to think that she and her husband were doing okay, even though they both commute to jobs and their only child is in day care most of the time.

She didn't want to admit that they needed more money. She did not want anything to do with owning her own business or with selling products or anything like that.

It's common for people to respond to opportunity with doubt and fear. Most people have very low self-esteem, and they don't believe they could do something different—much less something great—with their lives.

One month later, she was really excited about a new hair care product that she had purchased at her salon. She came to our house and told my wife all about the product, how good it was, how well it worked, how much it cost, and she even left the product as a sample overnight!

Was she selling? You bet.

Did she make any money when we bought the product from the salon on the basis of her enthusiastic testimonial? Not even a dime.

She was selling and didn't even know it!

My point is that people do this all the time. We tell each other about a good book, a great movie, a new restaurant. In fact we're always promoting something.

One day a neighbor stopped her car in front of my house to tell me that the local market was having a terrific sale on chickens and that we should hurry down there and get some before they sold out. She was selling chickens for them! And not making any money for her effort, either.

This is exactly what independent distributors do in the "B" system. They tell other people about a different, new and improved way to buy quality products and services that will save them money; and if they in turn want to spread the word, they can make money, too.

Here's what professor and author of *Unlimited Wealth*, Paul Zane Pilzer, said:

"The future in retailing—not only in Network Marketing—is in education. The greatest opportunities in our economy today and at least into the next decade, will be in the distribution sector rather than in the manufacturing sector, because in distribution we have yet to apply so much of the technology that we've applied to manufacturing.

"Within distribution, as evidenced by Home Depot, Amway, Nordstrom's, the companies that succeed will be the ones that concentrate on educating customers about new products and services that will improve their lives, even more than the companies who concentrate on finding a better way to physically distribute the product from manufacturer to consumer that the consumer already knows he or she wants. The Walmarts and Kmarts have already been there.

"Network Marketing today holds the greatest promise of any marketing innovation for accomplishing the goal of educating consumers about new products and services."

Let's say you become an independent distributor with a Network Marketing company that distributes certain types of products or services that you already buy and use. You can save about 30 percent by purchasing those products or services through the Network.

Then, you tell some other people about the "B" system, and you show them how to save 30 percent, and they start buying their products or services through the Network, also. And you tell a few others, and they tell some people, and before you know it, there are dozens or hundreds of people who are consistently buying through your Network. You created that sales volume—and you are rewarded for creating that volume.

Did you go out and sell products and drop off samples or anything like that?

No. You just shared some information.

You can retail the products if you want to, but that's not the best way to create volume. That's business as usual. You don't have enough time to move enough products to make very much money at the 30 percent markup. The money is in building a Network of distributors who are their own best customers.

In addition to the savings, the manufacturer will also pay you a commission of three to 25 percent of the total dollar volume that you and your Network create.

Let's say you've been in the Network for a while.

You've created a large word-of-mouth business just by sharing information and by teaching people what you know and showing them how to get involved.

You receive a 25 percent rebate on that total sales volume. The manufacturer pays you an additional 10 percent performance bonus for creating a certain level of volume of products and services in the Network. The rebates and bonuses are all set forth on a sliding scale that applies to everyone in the Network.

Let's add it up.

30 percent savings on products you bought for your own use, *plus*
25 percent rebate on the volume in your Network, *plus*
10 percent bonus for additional volume and performance, *equals*

65 percent total in savings, rebate and bonus

The manufacturer paid you the 65 percent that it was saving by not having a string of middlemen—by selling directly to its distributors who are also its primary customers.

Of course, not everyone who gets involved in the Network wants to talk to people and build a large business. Many people get involved just for the savings and the quality products. Most people who join the Network never sponsor anyone or build a business. So, the manufacturer is a very profitable company because, in most cases, it keeps most of the 65 percent that it saves by cutting out middlemen.

However, the manufacturer wants you to earn as much money as possible, because when you do that means more sales volume, and that means more profit for everyone. The manufacturer is required by the FTC to pay out as much as 66 percent of sales in bonuses to its distributors, sharing the profits.

Saving 30 percent is one good reason to get involved in a Network Marketing opportunity.

Earning extra money is a better reason.

Being able to buy unique, quality products is another reason.

More people are getting into Network Marketing because of the convenience, also.

How would you like to have the consumer products you use regularly delivered to your home whenever you need them?

If you could order all those consumer products in your bathroom, kitchen, pantry, medicine cabinet, laundry room, garage, and closets just by making one "800" phone call, and you knew you were getting top quality with a money-back guarantee and a 30 percent savings, would you shop that way?

More people are doing it. It saves you time and money.

Do you really care where you buy your cosmetics, toothpaste, paper towels, motor oil, socks, shampoo or vitamins, as long as they are of the quality and value that you demand?

Could you change your buying habits and tell some people about Network Marketing if it meant earning an extra $2000 or more a month?

Sure you could.

More Americans are shopping by television, computer, and telephone, buying what they want quickly and efficiently. Shopping is still a popular pastime, but going shopping downtown or to the mall is not. When you shop at home from catalogs, you avoid the traffic, the parking, the crime, and all the other hassles. Retail sales in shopping centers are down. Consumer shopping from home with credit cards is up. The number of consumers using on-line computer services for shopping is exploding. Pick up the phone and dial the "800" number and place your order, and your products are at your door in two days.

You just have to change your buying habits and plan ahead a couple of days. Most people wait until they run out of something, and then they hurry to the store to buy more, and they also impulsively buy other stuff that they didn't need, and that's why shopping that way is so expensive.

Plan, save time, save money.

Could you change your buying habits for the opportunity to earn an extra $2000 a month?

The "B" system ties into home shopping, home delivery, and wholesale buying trends.

For example; as a distributor you could buy a brand-name washing machine through your Network Marketing supplier. You order the appliance at a savings of 30 percent compared to the local retailer's price, and your supplier has the appliance "drop-shipped" to you directly from the maker of the washing machine.

It travels directly from the manufacturer's warehouse to you, the consumer, eliminating all of the traditional middlemen.

Industry analysts predict that 50 to 75 percent of all consumer products and services will be available through Network Marketing—the "B" system—by the end of the 1990s.

The "B" system spells death for the traditional middlemen, the people who used to control the product information and the product and the customer.

How much money can you make as an independent distributor with your own no-limit, high-leverage, Network Marketing business?

As much as you want.

Six-figure incomes are common for people who have steadily worked their businesses on a part-time basis for two to five years.

Would you have more options if you had an extra $100,000 a year coming in?

Professionals in Network Marketing are careful not to promise or exaggerate income claims, but there are many people making very large six-figure and low seven-figure residual incomes in this industry.

There are more millionaires in Network Marketing companies than in other, business-as-usual companies.

One distributor whose business is ten years old now earns a high, six-figure to low, seven-figure income; when he was asked how much he earned in his first year, he answered, "I don't really know because they're still paying me for it." That's residual income on past effort. You can create it, too.

It's not a "get rich quick" deal, though. It takes time, and you have to duplicate the success system and then teach that system successfully to others. Lone rangers and innovators have a tough time in Network Marketing. It's a team effort, as we will show in Chapter Eight.

Who is involved in Network Marketing?

Just to name a few: AT&T, Sprint, MCI, CocaCola, Gillette, Colgate-Palmolive, Chrysler, Ford, GMC, VISA, Sony, Sanyo, Texas Instruments, B.F. Goodrich, Sunbeam, Seiko, General Electric, Nikon, Canon, Nike, Coleman, Quaker Oats, and hundreds of others representing thousands of products and services.

These companies have found that person-to-person marketing is powerful. Network Marketing gets people together, and it gets people talking about products. It encourages spontaneous, voluntary testimonials about the quality of the products and the integrity of the company. Network Marketing creates a priceless form of advertising: unsolicited word-of-mouth.

Who are some of the names in Network Marketing?

Just to name a few: Tupperware, Watkins, Fuller Brush, Avon, Primerica, Amway Corporation, ServiceMaster, NuSkin International, Princess House, Rexall's Showcase International, Shaklee, Discovery Toys, Network 2000, Jaffra Cosmetics, Mary Kay Cosmetics, Reliv', Herbalife, Nanci, Cell Tech, Melaleuca, Oxyfresh, BodyWise, Lite & Rite, Enviro-Tech, PEP International, Japan Life, Liberty Call International, InVivo, Sunrider, and approximately 2,000 more companies that are growing fast internationally.

Network Marketing goes way beyond the other ways of leveraging time in a business. It has two major advantages over franchising and chain stores with employees.

1) Everyone you meet is a prospective distributor, because the cost to become involved is very low and no experience is required.

2) Everyone who becomes part of the Network can expand the business, so the potential for growth and profitability is unlimited. A modern Network Marketing business requires none of the risks, headaches, problems or limitations associated with "business as usual."

The History Of Network Marketing

The first Network Marketing plan was invented for a vitamin company called Nutrilite in 1945 by two Californians, Lee Mytinger and William Casselberry. They found they could pay sales people not only for their own sales but also on the sales of those they sponsored into the Network.

They found they could eliminate advertising by creating word of mouth through their independent distributors.

They also found they could eliminate expensive distribution middleman costs. Their customers were their distributors.

Two Nutrilite distributors, Rich DeVos and Jay Van Andel in Ada, Michigan, left Nutrilite to form Amway in 1959 with two cleaning products, SA-8 and LOC, and they bought out Nutrilite in 1972.

Amway has since become one of the most dramatic success stories in America. In 1994, the two low-profile owners of Amway, DeVos and Van Andel, were worth $2.7 billion apiece, according to *Forbes* magazine.

The Network Marketing industry has had to defend itself against a huge public misconception and a very poor image. Just like franchising in its early days, Network Marketing has been confused with fraudulent pyramid schemes. Amway, the pioneer in the industry, was hit the hardest by the media and the Federal Trade Commission (FTC).

In 1979, Amway won its four-year court case with the FTC, proving that Network Marketing is a legal business opportunity, not a pyramid scam.

In the ten years after that decision, the FTC and the Attorneys General in every state agreed on guidelines for deciding what is a legitimate Network Marketing business—and what is not.

Illegal pyramid scams squeeze large entry fees out of new members and don't deliver valuable products.

Reputable Network Marketing companies make money solely by selling valuable products and services.

The Duplication Principle

Duplicate your time through other people. It's the most powerful way to leverage your time. The reason Network Marketing is the most advanced concept in business today is that it allows geometric growth. Here is how the duplication idea can work for you.

The first step is to get started part-time and become your own best customer.

Then, set a goal and make a plan to spend six hours a week building your business. Sponsor six people into your business, and let's assume that they can each spend six hours each week building their Networks, with your help. You help each of your six to sponsor and train four new distributors. Then, help each of those four to sponsor two.

That's 78 people in your business.

Will the Network stop growing?

No. It will continue to grow because you trained the people in your Network to do the same things you learned to do. The Network keeps expanding, and you spend six hours a week helping the ones who want help.

You have multiplied your time through your Network of 78 people.

You are investing six hours a week in your business.

Your Network of 78 business associates each invests six hours a week—that's 468 hours.

You will receive a commission check, a bonus, on your share of the total volume of products and services created by the 468 hours of work.

And you only worked six hours that week!

The principle works the same way for everyone else in the Network, too. In fact, it is possible for you to earn more money than your sponsor. Someone you introduced to the business can build a larger business than yours, and you would be delighted, because, unlike in business as usual, it's not competitive. It's teamwork. It's profitable. When the people in your group are profitable, you are profitable. And you don't make any money until they do.

The word "duplicate" comes from the Latin word *duplicare*, meaning to double. Here's how it works.

The water hyacinth is a floating aquatic plant that starts out very small, but grows rapidly. In fact, its growth doubles daily, until one day, it covers 50 percent of the lake's surface area.

The next day—just 24 hours later—the plant covers the entire surface of the lake.

This doubling principle is a powerful idea.

Take one penny and double it every day for one month. How much money would you have?

Tomorrow you will have two cents, four cents the next day, eight cents the next day. By the end of the first week, you would have 64 cents.

At the end of the second week, you will have $81.92.

At the close of the third week, your original penny will be worth over $10,000.

In one month, you would have over ten million dollars.

That's an interesting image, and it applies to your Network Marketing business.

No, you won't make five million the first month, that's not the idea. But over five or ten years, if you keep doubling the number of people in your Network each year or every other year—which is very possible—your Network would include tens of thousands of people worldwide. It would be producing a prodigious volume of products and services. Your share would be an enormous residual income. It's not just theoretical. Many people just like you have developed this kind of business and residual income.

Start with yourself. Change your buying habits. Duplicate your time and energy through others by investing your time in other people. Create volume in your Network by teaching others how to build the business. Keep doing the same thing, persistently and consistently. It will be possible for you to enjoy a substantial, six-figure, residual income in two to five years.

That's not a promise—but it is a definite possibility. Many others have done it, and if just one other person can do it, then you can do it, too.

Your residual income will be based on the ongoing volume of products and services purchased internationally by tens of thousands of people in your Network, and you might never get to meet most of them. You will never see or touch most of the products moving through your Network. Independent shipping companies deliver the products to the distributors downline in your Network for you.

What About Saturation?

What happens when everyone gets in and the last guy in doesn't have anyone to sponsor and there's no one to sell to?

Theoretically, the whole world would be in your Network Marketing business if you kept doubling the number of people getting in. This widely held myth of saturation is a major stumbling block to the widespread public acceptance of Network Marketing.

In the early days of franchise growth, the same fear of saturation was vocalized by legislators trying to outlaw franchising. Saturation has not occurred in the franchising industry over a period of 25 years.

Market saturation is not possible in any market.

What about refrigerators? Doesn't every home already have one? Isn't that market saturated?

Not according to an appliance industry trade association, which announced that 1992 was the best year in two decades for refrigerator sales. Apparently, it didn't matter that everyone in America already had one. People wanted bigger ones, smaller ones, different colored ones, newer, better, whatever.

No market has ever been saturated. Markets change and shift and innovate, but they never get saturated.

Amway, the pioneer and giant of Network Marketing, started back in 1959, enough time to saturate the world and experience a plateau in growth.

Guess what? In 1992 it was still growing. In fact, in 1992 it grew by $1 billion over its 1991 sales, for a total of $4 billion in sales. Amway says it now has only one percent of the sales in any given market.

Today, Amway's sales are approaching $6 billion worldwide and the company projects sales of $10 billion before the end of the 1990s. Even with two million distributors, its rate of growth isn't even keeping up with the rate of new high school graduates in this country.

Americans move around, change jobs, change situations. Companies change and innovate products, and so you have this constant mixing and moving. People are born; they die; their situations change; immigrants arrive.

If saturation were a real threat, then it would have happened already, not just in Network Marketing, but in any industry.

Someone told me one time, "Oh, that. Everyone is already in." But it just isn't true. It's an excuse made by someone who doesn't want to participate in the opportunity right now.

Let's study a real Network Marketing plan. This is a conservative example of how you can earn an extra $2000 a month over the next six to 18 months. Nobody is promising you $2000 a month, but many people have done it, and, as I've said before, if just one person has done it, then you can do it, too.

The reason that residual income in Network Marketing is so reliable and stable is that the average distributor spends $200 a month on consumer products and services that they have to buy someplace every month. Given that the Network offers quality, savings, convenience, and the opportunity to make money, people keep buying the things they need every month from their own business. They keep sharing the idea.

Your Network Marketing business will consist of a lot of people each spending a little bit of money every month. Not one of them is a super salesperson.

Step One

Using the guidelines set forth in the next chapter, choose a Network Marketing opportunity that offers its distributors attractive discounts on quality products and/or services that you already use. Change your buying habits and start shopping through the Network, i.e., start buying from your own business.

Assume that you already spend around $200 each month on consumable products and services. You already buy them somewhere. So, you're not going to be purchasing any more than you already buy.

It doesn't matter how much or how little you spend, because there are no minimum purchases or quotas. Just for this example, assume you are an "average" family already spending $200 a month at your local stores.

As the following example shows, just by changing your buying habits and shopping through the Network, you will enjoy a 30 percent wholesale discount and earn a small three percent bonus check on your purchases. It adds up to $66 in savings and rebates. So, you are $66 ahead this first month—just by changing your buying habits.

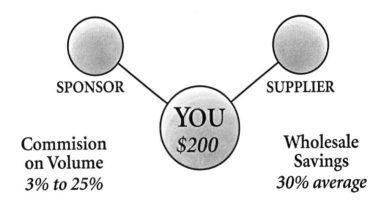

SPONSOR   SUPPLIER

YOU
$200

Commision   Wholesale
on Volume   Savings
3% to 25%   30% average

$6.00 commission (3% x $200)
+ $60.00 savings (30% x $200)
$66.00 immediate monthly profit

Diagram 12: Commission on Volume & Wholesale Savings

Step Two

Introduce others to the Network. Just tell them about this unique business idea. Show them how to save time shopping through the Network and how to save 30 percent on the products and services that they already are buying somewhere else.

Teach them how to order through the Network and train them to duplicate the success system.

In this particular example, you take their orders personally, make sure they receive their products, and pay them a bonus check out of your bonus check each month. They can also order and receive products and services directly from the supplier.

Let's say you invest six to 10 hours a week in people, sharing this idea. In two or three months, you will have signed up, or sponsored, six people into your Network. These people want to duplicate what you are doing, saving time and money and telling others about an exciting idea.

In the third month you will have earned $150 profit in this conservative example.

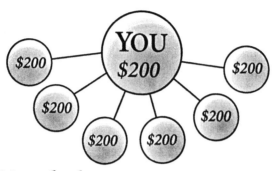

$1400 total volume

$126.00 commission (9% x $1400)
+ $60.00 savings
$186.00 immediate monthly profit
− $36.00 (Six $6.00 checks paid out)
$150.00 profit

Diagram 13: Commission on Volume

Step Three

Work with the six business associates you sponsored into your Network. Help them to share this business idea with others, and teach each of the six to sponsor four people. You only work directly with your six distributors, and they take care of their distributors.

You have a financial interest in building the depth of your Network, because you make money only when the people in your Network make money. So you help to share the idea with new people and help train them. You will be investing only six to ten hours a week.

In four to five months, your Network will have grown to 30 distributors. They are all duplicating the success system, buying through the Network, sharing the idea, and retailing a few products to people who ask for them. Assume all six of your associates do the same volume in this average example. Your profit is now $816 this month and you did not increase your time or effort in your business. You leveraged your time, and it is profitable. Your business looks like this:

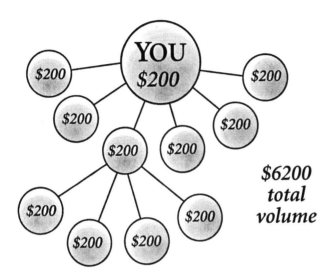

$6200
total
volume

$1116.00 commission (18% x $6200)
+ $60.00 savings
$1176.00 immediate monthly profit
− $360.00 (Six $60.00 checks paid out)
  $816.00 profit

Diagram 14: Commission on Total Volume

Step Four

Help each of your four newest distributors to sponsor two new associates. Invest six to 10 hours a week sharing this business concept and training your new distributors to duplicate the proven system.

You continue to build your own width, and by now, six to 18 months later, you have personally sponsored 20 to 30 people, not just the six. You also continue to work in depth in your business, helping to bring new people into the business, and you now have a Network of 78 people, all spending only about $200 a month in the Network.

At this level in the business, you place your orders directly with the corporation, instead of with your sponsor. And you receive products and your bonus checks directly from the corporation.

Your Network is creating over $15,000 a month in sales volume, and your profit on that volume is over $2000 a month.

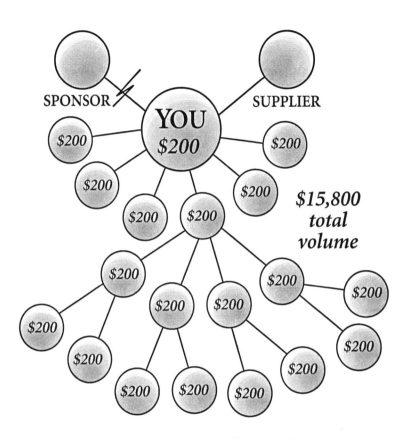

SPONSOR

SUPPLIER

YOU
$200

$200 (×18)

$15,800
total
volume

$3950.00 commission (18% x $6200)
+ $60.00 savings
$4010.00 immediate monthly profit
− $1872.00 (Six $60.00 checks paid out)
$2138.00 profit

Diagram 15: Commission on Total Volume

Step Five

Two to five years later, you have helped six of the distributors in your Network achieve the same level of volume that you achieved in step four. When those six distributors break away from your business, you get your time back and the corporation pays you a four percent bonus check on their total sales volume—forever.

This is permanent residual income for as long as there is volume flowing through their Networks. And the volume will keep growing, too, because more, new ambitious people are motivated to continue to build their businesses and to pursue their dreams.

Your total business income is now over $70,000 a year.

You continue to maintain your monthly commission income based on the sales volume in your personal Network, and you also receive the residual income on the volume of all those distributors you sponsored who became direct distributors with the corporation.

You now have a full-time income on a part-time effort.

How big can it get?

How big can you dream?

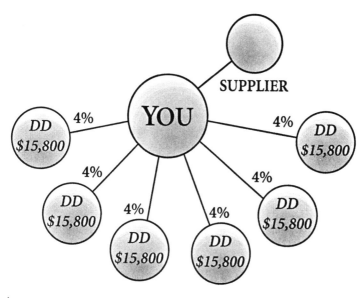

$15,800 x 4% = $632
$632 x 6 = $3,792
$3792 x 12 mo. = $ 45,500 4% royalty income
$2138 x 12 mo. = $25,656 3% to 25% commission
                    $71,156 total annual income

Diagram 16: Commission on Total Volume

CHAPTER 5
Checklist for Choosing a Company

O wning your own traditional business can be a frightening thing to think about. We've all heard about the high failure rates for new businesses. 80 percent of them fail in their first year. Worse, of the businesses that survive their first year, three out of five do not last five years, much less 10. How many 10-year-old companies do you do business with?

Why such a high failure rate? Lots of reasons.

Two of the most common reasons for failure are:

1) Starting the business without enough money to get it going. Or . . .

2) Not having the expertise or a proven system to follow—i.e., not having anyone to teach you how to be successful.

Getting rich is easy. Finding someone who can teach you how and who will help you is the hard part. It doesn't happen very often in the world of business as usual.

Your boss or manager doesn't want you to know as much as he or she knows, because then you would be a threat to their power and security.

But with your own Network Marketing business, things are different. You will be in business for yourself, but not by yourself. You will have a team of experts, successful people ahead of you, who are willing and able to teach you the business.

Ambitious individuals who follow the guidelines in this book and who follow the proven success system and plan of action, those who put in the required part-time effort consistently and persistently and don't quit— those businesses are successful.

Over the past 30 years, Networking Marketing companies have come and gone. Many suddenly appeared, only to disappear just as fast. As many as 90 percent of all new corporate Network Marketing start-ups fail in the first year. That's higher than the failure rate for new conventional businesses.

However, independent Networking Marketing distributors do not fail when they duplicate a proven success system. They have 100 percent success when they build their Network Marketing businesses with an established, solid, successful supplier. The supplier must be a manufacturer of quality, competitive products with a proven support organization that provides ongoing training and motivation for its distributors.

The new companies that fail usually have a limited line of products. They make wild claims about their compensation plan and income potential and the quality of their products. Many run afoul of the Federal Trade Commission.

Be sure the company has been around long enough to be established. Talk to some people who have been involved with the company.

Have they ever missed a bonus check?

Do they receive their orders quickly?

Do they ship directly to their distributors?

How long has the company has been in business? Does the company stand behind its products?

What kind of training and support is available?

Does the company produce professional promotional materials?

Would you continue using the products for the rest of your life—regardless of the business opportunity?

A company that pushes the idea that timing is everything and that "you need to get in now" is suspect. The opportunity needs to be just as good many years from now as it is today, or your long-term prospects are dim.

New companies often claim to be on a wave. They say there is a limited window of opportunity, so you need to get in now at the beginning, near the top. They are implying that the business won't be quite as good for the others who will get in later. That's short-term thinking.

You want to build a business that will continue to grow forever.

You need a strong, committed supplier that will be around years from now.

Check out the people who own the company.

What is their background?

Have they hopped around in the Network Marketing industry?

Or have they dedicated themselves to manufacturing and distributing quality products and services?

Have they committed themselves to creating a long-term opportunity for entrepreneurs to own their own businesses?

Are they committed to the success of their distributors?

Look for a company that has active distributor organizations for training, support and motivation.

Is the company committed to expanding internationally? Are they established in other countries? Can you build an international Network Marketing business?

Is the company committed to environmentally sound products, packaging, and practices? Those are important concerns for many customers and entrepreneurs.

Get involved with a manufacturer of consumer products and services that people buy, use, and buy again. That way you have repeat sales volume in your business, month in and month out. That creates dependable, reliable, residual income.

If you have to sell new customers every month, because you have only one product and people don't buy a replacement for a long time, that's business as usual. There's little potential to develop residual income that way.

If you need to become an expert on complicated or specialized products, then you'll spend all your time explaining the products to people, trying to prove to them why they should be using them. (If your products are unique and new enough that they require explanation, make sure your company does the explaining for you—accompanying sales literature, audios and videos should do that job for you. You're not here to become a product specialist.)

On the other hand, if you know that your prospects already use or are interested in using products like those you represent, then you can easily offer them a way to purchase similar or better products at a discount through your Network. And you can show them the business opportunity at the same time.

Coca-Cola became very rich when they started using some of the first vending machines. Every gas station had one. Every store porch had one. Each vending machine produced only a little bit of volume, but the company had thousands of them scattered across the country.

Think of your potential Network as a business with thousands of locations each doing just a little bit of volume. Picture thousands of families in your Network each buying just $100 to $200 worth of products each month through the Network. And they do that every month. And they tell others how to save money on quality products and how to make money, too, through the Network.

When you have that kind of business, you have a large residual income. That's the kind of business that can give you a six-figure income for the rest of your life—and keep growing even when you decide to stop building the business.

The best products and services to be involved with are basic household products and services that everyone buys and uses every month. Avoid the Network Marketing company that offers only one or two products, especially if they are one-time purchases. Look for a company that distributes valuable consumer products and services that are unique and competitively priced. Avoid a company if their brands can be purchased cheaper at Walmart, Costco or Price Club.

Beware of the little company with only one product; it might be difficult to create very much volume, no matter what their claims for future growth may be.

Be suspicious of the brand new company that says you need to get in right now on the "ground-floor"; they're thinking short-term. Watch out for the company that does not manufacture its own products; they are primarily a middleman.

Beware of promises of fantastic future growth. Watch out for promises that they will be adding more products or opening in other countries. Evaluate the opportunity based on what the company offers today—not what they say it is going to be later.

Also avoid the manufacturer or distributor organization that leans heavily on a certain morality or political view for its identification or major purpose. If the leaders at the seminars are telling you how to vote or how you are going to save America by being involved in the business, they have overstepped the boundaries of business.

I'm all for supporting a high standard of ethics in business and family life. A long-term business must be built on honesty and integrity and other ethical values.

But when the leaders in a business peddle their own moral or religious values, the chances of turning off new prospects are very high. You are looking for a no-limit business opportunity that stands on its own with valuable products and services and a fair and rewarding compensation plan for your time and efforts.

Find out if the company has ever been or is currently under investigation by the Federal Trade Commission (FTC), the Internal Revenue Service (IRS) or the Food and Drug Administration (FDA).

To find out, call the Direct Selling Association at (202) 293-5760 in Washington, D.C. or the MultiLevel Marketing International Association in Irvine, CA at (714) 854-0484.

"Is It Legal?"

How do you make sure the company is a legitimate Network Marketing opportunity?

There is no Federal Trade Commission definition of a legal Network Marketing company, but in 1979 the FTC set a precedent when it ruled that Amway Corporation was legal because it met the following criteria. These parameters have become the standards of the industry:

1) The corporation does not pay distributors to recruit people.

2) Distributors receive bonus checks based on the volume of products and services sold to other distributors and to retail customers.

3) There is an unconditional 100 percent money-back guarantee on products, services and promotional materials

4) No initial purchase of inventory is required, and no minimum orders or quotas are required to participate in the Network.

5) There is no way to buy your way into the Network at a higher bonus level. Everyone starts at the beginning. The opportunity is the same for everyone.

6) Valuable, competitive (and competitively priced), unique products are distributed to wholesale and retail customers through the distributors in the Network.

7) There is a profit motive to build the business. The products and services have value regardless of the incentives or profitability of the marketing plan.

8) The only initial "up front" requirements for getting started are reasonable fees to cover the administrative sign-up process and necessary start-up materials.

"Is It a Pyramid?"

First, what is a pyramid? There are three kinds:

1) The Mayans and Egyptians built some really good ones. They are pointed at the top and wide at the bottom. Many are still standing. It's a good design.

2) Every large corporation and small business with employees is a pyramid. It has a chairman or president at the top and a bunch of workers across the bottom with managers and officers filling in the middle, pointed at the top and wide across the bottom.

3) Ponzi schemes and chain letters are examples of fraudulent pyramids, the kinds some people mistakenly associate with Network Marketing. This kind of pyramid looks like a business, but the owner takes money from people and gives them nothing of value in return, just the promise of something for nothing, the promise of getting rich quickly.

The new people in a fraudulent pyramid have to defraud some other people to get their money back. When somebody blows the whistle and the cops show up, the bad guys at the top split with all the money, if they can get away, and the people at the bottom lose all their money.

In a fraudulent pyramid, no valuable, competitive products or services are distributed to customers. Money is made by recruiting other people, who must in turn recruit others to get their money back. Two highly publicized pyramid scams busted by the Federal Trade Commission and the District Attorney were FundAmerica and Holiday Magic.

In a legitimate Network Marketing opportunity, the pyramid structure is temporary. Every new distributor can build the business to a level of volume where he or she works directly as an independent contractor with the corporation. That breaks the temporary tie, or apprenticeship, with their sponsor for products and bonus checks.

There is a growing trend in the industry today to bypass the traditional method of ordering and receiving products from your sponsor. Many new companies take orders directly from a new distributor and ship directly as well, which relieves the sponsor of the detail of physically handling orders and products and record keeping.

It remains to be seen if the Federal Trade Commission and the Attorney General will view this as a distributor Network or a sponsoring game. It may be enough if the compensation is based on sales volume of products and services in the distributor's Network, regardless of whether the distributor physically handles those orders. One of the requirements for a valid distributorship in Network Marketing is that the business supplies wholesale and retail customers with products and services.

Two trade associations represent the Network Marketing industry:

Multi-Level Marketing International Association (MLMIA)
119 Stanford Court Irvine, CA 92715 (714) 854-0484

Direct Selling Association
1776 K Street Washington, D.C. 20006 (202) 293-5760

Both of these organizations maintain lists of member companies and the categories of products and services they manufacture.

Request their member lists, so you can contact the suppliers and manufacturers involved in the areas of Network Marketing that offer the best opportunities.

Request information from those that interest you, according to the guidelines set out in this book.

The trade associations also follow up on complaints and tend to be aware of companies that may be under investigation or that may have problems that you would want to know about if you were considering getting involved with them.

At this writing, I am not aware of any truly impartial industry source offering objective advice or recommendations of sound, Network Marketing opportunities. You will need to take the information in this book and apply it as you investigate Network Marketing companies. After reading this book you will be capable of making your own well-informed choice.

Ultimately, you want a company that you feel comfortable with, a company that you trust. You want to be involved with products and services that you trust and can get excited about. You want an unlimited compensation plan that is simple to understand and explain—and one that will reward you richly for your efforts.

Success magazine and *Entrepreneur* magazine are both available at newsstands. Both publications have been covering the Network Marketing industry. Other business and opportunity magazines also feature regular articles about Network Marketing.

Consider what owning your own no-limit, high-leverage, Network Marketing business can offer you:

It offers unlimited, dependable income that produces financial security.

It offers long-term, increasing cash flow and enhanced quality of life.

It offers the tax advantages legally available to businesses.

It offers the potential of a balanced success in all the important areas of life.

In other words, a Network Marketing business offers cash flow, the opportunity to have the money to make investments, desirable tax advantages, and discretionary time—all of the elements of real wealth.

What are some other things to consider when choosing a Network Marketing business opportunity?

Here is a review of the qualities that an ideal business opportunity would need to offer in order for anyone to be able to get involved and become successful.

1) It would need to be legal and ethical. Period.

2) It would provide positive recognition for your effort.

3) It would provide a good return on the time you invest in it. It would offer the potential, but not the promise, of a large, six-figure income in two to five years, over and above your primary source of income. It would be a "cash business" with no accounts receivable owed to you.

4) It would require very nominal capital investment, minimum time requirement, no investment and limited risk. It would need to be something you could start on a part-time, flexible basis, say six to 10 hours a week, and something you could get into for a one-time investment of just a few hundred dollars, at most.

5) It would offer the potential for financial independence. It would be the kind of business that you could continue to build, at your own pace, forever. You would never need to retire from it, and so you would not need to worry about retirement.

6) It would have negligible overhead expenses, if any. It could be started and operated from your home without any special equipment or inventory. It would not require employees. It would not require special licenses or extensive training.

7) It would offer permanent, self-sustaining income—residual income, whether you continued to actively build the business or not. The ongoing residual (or "royalty") income would continue for as long as there was sales volume in your Network. It would give you a "walk-away" income; that is, you could walk away from the business and your income would not be affected, because the volume of products and services moving through your Network would continue to grow.

8) It would have no territory or geographic franchise limitations. It could grow and expand anywhere. It would be a portable business in the sense that you could move and live virtually anywhere in the free world and continue to build your business. It would offer unlimited growth potential.

9) It would have to be compatible with your current primary business or occupation. It would produce a diversified income, so that if something ever happened to you or to your primary source of income you would not be hurt financially. It would have the potential to produce a far greater income than your primary income.

10) It would offer the opportunity to be involved with associates of recognized integrity, people with whom you enjoy working and playing. It would offer the opportunity to meet new people and make new friends and business associates.

11) It would offer the legitimate tax advantages that are available to all businesses, so that a percentage of all your business activities and expenses, including travel, could be deducted from your income taxes. It would require very little bookkeeping and accounting activities.

12) It would not be something seasonal, faddish, trendy or otherwise short-term. It would involve an association with an established supplier or manufacturer with a proven record of success.

13) It would have to be inflation-resistant. It would involve quality, competitive, consumer products and services that people need and buy over and over again.

14) It would offer the opportunity to travel around the country and the world.

15) It would include a support system, a team of experts who are successful in the same business, who have a financial and personal interest in helping you to succeed with a proven plan of action.

16) It would be capable of being shared with other people that you care about because you wouldn't want to keep something this good all to yourself. You could bring others into the business Network and teach them how to succeed. It would be a business in which anyone could be successful.

17) It would have to be a business that is inheritable, or transferable, so that your heirs or estate would get the benefit of your efforts. The equity that you build up and the residual income stream that you create could continue to grow forever to benefit whomever you want to leave it to.

18) And, finally, it would have to be fun and exciting.

If this all sounds impossible, it isn't. It's being done all the time.

People with less time, less talent and less ambition than you have are becoming wealthy in businesses that fit the description above.

It's done with time leveraging and duplication of effort to create a Network of people who together create a tremendous volume by purchasing products and services at wholesale discounts and sharing the idea with other people.

It is done by taking a little bit of your time—little windows or cracks of time, little bits here and there—on a flexible part-time basis, and investing that time with some other people who are doing the same thing. And by doing so, you can accomplish things financially that you could never do all by yourself.

The magic lies in your knowing—and letting others know—that *anyone can do it.*

Since anyone can get involved and become successful, your potential business growth and income is unlimited.

CHAPTER 6
The Eight-Step Success System

A successful Network Marketing business is based on a simple formula that anyone can duplicate. It is simple to follow and just as simple to teach. Following this two-to-five-year proven plan of action is as close to a guarantee of success as you will ever find in the world of business.

Duplicate this Eight-Step Success System and your Network Marketing business will grow. Teach the system to others and you can create unlimited freedom and wealth.

Many people have done it. You can do it, too.

Step One

BE YOUR OWN BEST CUSTOMER.

Buy the products and services from your own business.

Now, I don't mean that you should go out and buy things that you don't need. What I do mean is that instead of shopping for all your consumer products and services through the "A" system, change your buying habits and buy from the "B" system. And buy those products from your own business.

The first step to success in Network Marketing is to *change your buying habits* immediately. Stop relying on products and services from the "A" system. Remember, they're your competitors. Save time and money by ordering unique, quality products at wholesale discounts from your own business. Have them delivered directly to your home.

How soon after starting your business should you start using the products and services that are available through your Network?

It depends.

How fast do you want your business to grow?

Right away, probably.

When you use the products and services from your own business, you will have confidence and belief in them. You will be familiar with them. People will see that you buy from your own business. It will be easy and natural to share the products and the business opportunity with other people. When you are excited about the products and the business, people will respond positively to you.

Step Two

SHARE THE NETWORK MARKETING IDEA.

Show the concept to everyone you know.

You meet new people all the time. Focus your attention on other people, and offer them the opportunity to join you in your business. Then teach them to follow this proven, Eight-Step Success System. Help them to do what you do. Duplicate your effort by investing your time in others to help them get what they want.

Loan them this book. Better yet, have them get their own copy.

Look for positive, ambitious, open-minded people. Remember that everyone is a prospect, regardless of whether you think they might or might not be interested. They will be interested when they know what you know.

There's a wonderful expression of this truth you can tell people that will help them grasp the perspective you're offering:

If you knew what I know about this business, nothing in heaven or on Earth would stop you from getting involved right now.

Often the busiest, most successful people are the best prospects. They are quick to understand and appreciate concepts such as diversification and residual income. See yourself building a marketing team of people. See yourself teaching new distributors this simple Eight-Step Success System.

A) Make a list of people whom you would like to invite into your business. Do not prejudge anyone. You never know who will be interested until you talk to them. Add to your list daily; you meet (and recall that you previously met) new people all the time.

B) Talk to at least one person on your list each day. Use the phone to get appointments.

C) Share the Network Marketing idea with new prospects at least three times a week. Your business needs new people to grow. Give them this book.

D) Set a goal to sponsor at least two new distributors a month into your own business. This growth is your business width. Many of these people will join the Network just to buy products and services at the wholesale discount. Many will have no interest in building a business. Width produces immediate profits.

E) Work with your distributors who want to build their business. Help them to duplicate this success system. Teach them to do what you do. Help them to sponsor and train new distributors. This growth is your business depth. Depth produces long-term financial security.

This sponsoring process is not a selling job. This is not the convincing business. Building your Network Marketing business is a process of finding out what people want and showing them a financial vehicle and a proven success system for getting what they want. It is a process of sorting through people to find the ones who are looking for a better way to live.

This business is about people helping people. It's a people business, not a product business. It's based on developing long-term business and social relationships, not on closing the sale. It's offering people a better way to live. We focus on the people, not on the products.

Professional sales people sometimes have a difficult time with this idea. They sometimes have to unlearn many of the short-term activities that are common practices in conventional business as usual.

Let me explain this once again, because it really is a different slant on things than most people expect: This is *not really a "products business,"* even though your income is based on the volume of products you create. This business is a *relationship business.*

It is not about talking and convincing; it is about listening to people, finding out what they want, and showing them a way to get what they want, and then working with them and helping them get their goals.

Step two is about "S.T.P."

See The People;
Share The Plan;
Sell The Products;
Sponsor The Prospects;
Supply/Teach/Pay;
Spend The Profits.

Many people have done it. You can do it, too.

Step Three

SELL SOME PRODUCTS.

Network Marketing is a wholesale/retail business opportunity. Your Network Marketing business is not a wholesale buying club. Even though your business will be only five percent retail to customers and 95 percent wholesale to other distributors in your Network, retailing is an important part.

Most states have specific requirements and licenses governing wholesale buying clubs, and Network Marketing companies are a different category of business.

This is not to say you should to go door to door and sell products. Please don't do that! It doesn't work.

That was the old way. Do not try to operate a minimart from your home. Do not pester your friends and family to buy products from your catalogs. This is not the idea. You do not have time for that, and even it you did have the time, the 30 percent average markup is not sufficient to make very much money. You would have to move boxcar loads of products yourself to make any significant money, and that would be "business as usual" with no time leverage.

When you share the Network Marketing business idea with people, most of them are not going to get involved right now. It would be great if they all did, but they don't.

Not everyone is looking.

Not everyone understands this business concept at first.

Not everyone is open to change and growth.

Not everyone is going to like what you have to say.

The idea is to offer to provide products at retail prices to the people who decide not to take advantage of the Network Marketing business opportunity.

Many of the people who say "No" to the business opportunity will want to become your "preferred customers." You can serve them by making sure they know how to order the products, by making sure they receive their products, and by making sure that you offer them the very best customer service.

Many of your preferred, retail customers eventually will join your Network when they learn more about the products, more about the business, and more about you. Retailing your products pays you immediately for your time.

The first three steps in this Eight-Step Success System deal with external things: using products, sponsoring people, and selling products.

Steps four through eight deal directly with you—the only thing over which you have total control. That's a critically important truth to remember, too, because it will keep you out of the trap of feeling at the mercy of your circumstances.

You have control over you. That's the key to dealing with everything else.

If you want to experience more success in life, you have to work on yourself. To improve your outer world, you need to first improve your inner world. When you get yourself right, your world will be right.

Step Four

READ BOOKS THAT CAN HELP YOU.

There is an entire library of books just waiting for you to read them. If you have already read them all, then reread them. It's amazing how much you'll learn the second or third time through. Read books on leadership, people skills, personal growth, self-improvement, success principles, and Network Marketing.

Many people quit reading when they quit going to school. Some people are trying to make their high school or college education last them through life.

Education is not a vaccination. It's ongoing. Formal schooling just gets you started. You need to keep reading and keep learning throughout your life. If you do not, you will be left behind, financially and socially. A person who does not read is in the same category as the person who never learned to read. Readers are leaders, and leaders are readers.

Read at least 15 minutes a night before going to bed. There is something powerful about filling the mind with positive, hopeful ideas and information. The subconscious mind works on the information all night while you sleep. In the morning, you're not the same person. You're starting to grow.

Start your reading program by reading one book a month. Then read a book every two weeks. Then read a minimum of a book a week.

Step Five

LISTEN TO MOTIVATIONAL AUDIO TAPES ON SUCCESS.

Listen to educational audio tapes in your field of interest.

Listen to success stories of other business people in Network Marketing.

Listen for their teaching.

Turn your car into a university on wheels. Depending how much you drive each week, you can get the equivalent of a full semester's worth of university lectures in several months. Instead of plugging in those music tapes or listening to the radio, turn on a seminar tape that can help you.

Remember, listening to motivational tapes on success can actually make you feel better. Medical science has proved that your body produces certain hormones when you are feeling optimistic and excited about your future, and those hormones actually make you feel better.

Tapes will give you ideas that will help you reach your goals faster.

You will learn to work with other people.

You will learn how to talk to other people, and how to listen.

Tapes give you access to experts who have studied for years, and you can listen to them while you do other things.

Listen to tapes when you are working in the kitchen, when you are working in the yard. Study the recorded seminar tapes of the leaders in your Network Marketing business if they are available.

Step Six

ATTEND SEMINARS AND CONVENTIONS THAT CAN HELP YOU.

The leaders in your distributor organization probably offer training seminars. The corporation that supplies you with products and services probably hosts conventions. Be there at any cost. Take some people with you. Take advantage of every opportunity to be around people who are more successful than you in your business. Learn to do what they did. Duplicate their actions. Duplicate their attitude and character. The idea is to learn what successful people do, and then do what they do.

Use a tape recorder.

Keep a pen and tablet with you and take notes.

Become a student of the business.

Earn while you learn.

Remain teachable and continue to learn. You'll never know enough, and you'll never know it all. And you'll never know when someone might share just the right bit of information that you need in order to move further along in your business.

Be yourself. Don't try to copy somebody else's personality or style. But the attitudes and activities of successful people are things you can learn to duplicate. When you do the things they did, you will enjoy the success they have.

Step Seven

ASSOCIATE WITH POSITIVE PEOPLE.

This includes both people in your business and those with whom you associate socially, outside your business.

Build quality relationships with people in your Network, with people you sponsor and with those who have been in the business longer than you have.

Research has shown that your income tends to be the average income of your 10 closest friends. Positive associations will have a tremendous impact on you.

Being around successful people is stimulating. Successful people are positive people. They cheer you on. They tell you that you can do it. They are excited about your success, and they're interested in helping you.

Step Eight

COUNSEL REGULARLY WITH YOUR SPONSOR OR ACTIVE LEADER UPLINE IN YOUR NETWORK.

Ask them to help you set realistic goals for building a solid business. Learn from those who have done it. Don't try to reinvent the wheel; that will cost you time and money.

Ask for help.

The leaders in your business are interested in your success. When you make money, they make money too. Be sure that you follow their direction and duplicate their actions. Learn to do the right things, right from the start.

Your leaders will be interested in helping you when you follow through by doing what you say you will do. They will be interested in what you do, not what you say you're going to do. You build trust and confidence when you do what you say you'll do. Trust must be earned by actions. Trust is very hard to regain once it is lost.

Three Cardinal Rules

1) Always check with your sponsor or the leaders in your Network—your upline—before you do anything for the first time.

It isn't that you have to ask permission, but you want to duplicate the activities that produce a successful business. If you innovate, you might mess up a proven system.

Innovation can destroy your business, because the people whom you've sponsored into your business will duplicate you, and if you are providing them with a poor example, your business will suffer.

You want a business Network of people who are all doing the profitable things that work. That way everybody makes money. Learn to do the things that work—right from the beginning.

2) Always be sure never to embarrass anyone.

The subconscious mind cannot take a joke. When you make fun of someone, they don't think it's funny. When you put the spotlight on someone in a critical way, it hurts them. The other people present in the group will secretly wonder if you're going to embarrass them next.

Lift people up instead. Be sincere. Make them feel good. Most people suffer from low self-esteem, even though most of us cover it up. If you can't say something positive and complimentary, bite your tongue.

3) Gossiping and complaining will kill your business.

If you have a challenge or a negative situation, take it to your sponsor or to the leaders in your Network. Chances are good that they have dealt with a similar situation in the past and will be able to help you to resolve the situation.

More Ideas That Work

Treat your business like a million-dollar business from the beginning, and it will become one.

Pretend you have invested $250,000 of your own money in it. Don't be fooled by the low cost of entry in Network Marketing. Just because it costs only a few hundred dollars at most to get started, that doesn't make it a pretend business or a hobby. It is capable of outperforming every other form of business in the world.

Network Marketing is a people business, not a product business.

You focus on people and their needs and feelings, not on the products. When you move the people, the products will move, too. But you cannot move the people by just moving products.

Get to know a good accountant.

Learn to save all receipts. Handle your business expenses to your advantage.

Creating legitimate tax advantages is one major reason to own a business. Almost every activity can be turned into a business activity. Every trip you take can be a business trip. Learn to generate business expenses. Take maximum advantage of the tax laws. Every dollar that you can write off your taxes is a dollar that you can spend on something else.

Hire an accountant and learn to use a chart of accounts.

Use the telephone to get appointments with people.

Use every meeting to set up another appointment.

After every appointment, ask yourself, "What did I do right?" and "How could I do better next time?"

People are going to say "No" to your business opportunity. They are not saying "No" to you. A "No" is a stepping stone to a "Yes." A "No" is not a rejection, not a failure, just another outcome or experience.

Not everyone is looking for an opportunity.

Not everyone thinks they can be successful.

Not everyone is ambitious.

Finding people who are open-minded, ambitious, and looking for a way to get their goals is like turning over the cards in a deck to find the aces. You know they are in there somewhere. The way you get them is by turning over all the cards until you find them. You'll find them, unless you quit looking.

Use the 80/20 rule.

Talk to 100 people and show them the opportunity to get their goals in Network Marketing. 80 of them might say "No." 20 will say "Yes." Don't worry about the ones who say "No," just keep looking for the aces in the deck.

Move quickly and sponsor 20 your first year. That's less than two a month. Out of the 20, seven will probably quit, seven will be good wholesale customers, three will hang around, and three will be hot to build their Network Marketing business now. Work with those three hot ones.

You can only work with three or four people at a time to build substantial depth in your business. The three that were hanging around will catch on later, and you can work with them and help them build their businesses when they are ready.

In your second year, go sponsor another 20. Develop another six (three hot ones and three hanging around) at a time. You'll have a huge business. People who have done this now have six-figure incomes for life, and that income can be willed to their kids or their estate.

Remember that everybody is important.

Nobody is under you or beneath you or above you in your line of sponsorship. The people you sponsor are on your team. Everybody in your group is on your team. Everyone is important.

There are no big shots in this business.

Every person is a pulse of energy with a unique story and special reasons for wanting to succeed. Find out what they want and show them how to get it. Help them set goals in their business and then work with them to achieve their goals.

By investing your time in people, you leverage your time—and when you leverage your time, you are *owning your future*.

Make a list of people.

Psychologists tell us that the average high school graduate knows about 800 people.

You meet new people all the time.

You know thousands of people.

You might not know all of their names.

You might not know very much about them. But there are people you see every day who recognize you. There are people from your clubs, schools, jobs, churches, family, friends, and all of the people with whom you have interacted over the years—thousands of them.

Start your list of people on paper. Don't even consider whether they'd be interested in a business or whether you'd be comfortable talking to them. The first step is simply to create a large list.

What will happen, as you work on this for days and weeks and months, is that when you remember one person it jogs your memory, and pretty soon, with practice, you are just overflowing with names of people that you didn't even know that you knew.

Write them all down.

Mailman, doctor, dentist, paperboy, minister, lawyer, accountant, insurance agent, pharmacist, veterinarian, optometrist, Congressman, barber, hair stylist, builder, real estate agent, mortgage broker, banker, teller, PTA president, golfing buddy, babysitter's parents, dry cleaner, UPS driver, travel agent, jeweler, librarian, printer, mechanic, waitress, policeman, next door neighbor, and on and on and on . . . you know a lot of people!

When you have developed your list, think about the individual people.

- Which ones live the closest to you?
- Who seem to be the most successful?
- Which ones are outgoing and ambitious?
- Who already owns a business or has a job in management?
- Which ones have families?

Call these people first and get an appointment to share some information with them. Just be yourself and show them something that you have discovered. Tell them why they might be interested, too. Tell them why you got involved.

You might want to just loan them this book. You probably have other materials from your sponsor or supplier, too. I built my business just by loaning people an early version of this book. Some read it; some didn't. Some got in the business; most of them did not.

I just kept putting the book into people's hands and kept asking if they were looking for other ways to make money. Enough people did get into the business and got excited about their future and built their own business.

Use a calendar/planner and keep it with you at all times.

Write your goals in it, and use it to schedule your priorities. Use every meeting to set up another appointment. Always leave someone knowing when you'll see them again, and why—or else you might spend days or weeks trying to catch up with them again.

Get involved in people's lives in a positive way.

Build bridges of understanding. Reach out to people. Be yourself. Give yourself away. Give your business away.

People usually talk about four things when they have conversations, especially when they are just getting to know each other.

Think of the word FORM; it's a useful acronym for asking meaningful questions.

F = FAMILY

Almost everyone has a family. If they don't have a family, they must be FROM somewhere. *"Do you have kids, too . . . ? Where are you from . . . ?"*

O = OCCUPATION

Most people work. They have a job or a business. *"I'm a waitress on the weekends, what kind of work do you do?"*

R = Recreation
People love to talk about their hobbies and their sports. *"Do you play golf?"*

M = Marketing Message
Tell them about what you do that has something in it for them. *"I'm involved in a profitable, wholesale/retail business where we save a lot of money, and we show other people how to do the same thing. Are you open to other ways of making money or are you pretty much committed to your job for the rest of your life?"*

Loan them this book and set an appointment to get it back in 24 to 48 hours. When you meet with them, answer their questions, share the Network Marketing idea with them, and show them the example of how to make an extra $2000 a month.

Some will join your business, some won't.

You are sorting though people to find the ones who are looking. You're turning over the cards to find the aces.

What does it mean to sponsor a new distributor into your Network?

It means helping them to obtain the necessary business startup kit from your supplier.

It means teaching them how to order and receive their products.

It means answering their questions and training them to follow the proven Eight-Step Success System, and making sure they begin to duplicate the things that you do.

It's getting to know them better.

It's learning to work with them, helping them to become a success in the business.

It's making a friend in the business.

Learn to answer the questions and objections that will come your way.

When people ask questions or have objections, that's great. They're interested. The most common questions (or objections) are these, or variations of the following:

I don't have time. I'm too busy.
My wife (husband) won't let me.
It's already saturated.
It's a pyramid.
I'm not a salesman.
I wouldn't be interested in anything like that.
We're doing okay.
We don't have the money to get started.

Learn to empathize with people.

These are simply excuses, usually based on fear and doubt. Most people have a concern for status, which is usually simply a poor self image. They have an intense fear of failure. They are afraid of change. They are afraid to talk to people. They just want you to show them that they can do this business, too.

One very effective way to answer objections is to use the "Feel, Felt, Found" formula.

You can say:

I know how you feel . . .
I felt the same way . . .
Then I found out some information that changed my mind . . . .

Be familiar with the information in this book, so you can share with people and help them overcome their excuses, fears and doubts. They want to believe they can do it. They want it to be true.

Who wouldn't want to improve their financial situation?

Who wouldn't want to be part of a winning team?

Who wouldn't jump at the chance to be successful, especially if there were someone to help them . . . especially if there were a team of experts, a support system and a proven Eight-Step Success System to follow?

When people have excuses, questions, objections, it's all the same thing. They want more information, they want you to show them that they can do it, too. They want to trust you. They'll be motivated by the depth of your conviction and enthusiasm—*not* by the force of your logic.

Share it, don't sell it. People don't care how much you know until they know how much you care.

Friendship is the key to this business. Friendship precedes profits.

Stick with it; know that it takes time.

Following the Eight-Step Success System and putting in the required action enthusiastically for six to eight weeks will generate consistent results in your business.

Another six months of consistent, persistent action will generate momentum. The momentum that you create in the first six months of your business will carry you through the two to five years that it takes to create lasting residual income in Network Marketing.

The leaders in your Network will make themselves known by their actions.

Help them set goals. Better to set high goals than low ones, but unrealistic goals kill motivation. It's better to set a series of goals, like stepping stones, so your next goal is just out of reach but not out of sight, and that way you'll be able to reach the really lofty ones.

Teach others to set goals, and work with the ones who want to grow. Be willing to stretch yourself and help others move further along, too. It's easier and more fun to run with a hundred than to try to drag one along with you.

Know that you'll need to give your full effort.

What's important enough for you to sweat blood and put yourself in uncomfortable situations?

You always have to pay full price in advance for success. There's no bargaining over the price. Efforts come before rewards. Sometimes you deposit the money in the north and then make withdrawals in the south. That is to say, 95 percent of your income will come from five percent of your effort. You'll never know which five percent are the ones that produce the 95 percent, so you have to keep putting in 100 percent effort.

Successful achievers learn to do the things failures will not do. They do what they need to do to get their goal, no matter what, whether they feel like doing it or not. They enhance the lives of other people. They live by values that they know to be right. They live by clear-cut ethics and moral standards.

Network Marketing is a win/win business.
Success in this business requires leaders who stay in the creative, productive stage. Leaders are cheerleaders, urging and nurturing champions with recognition.

Stay creative: keep building.
There are four possible stages in this business:

1) Creative;
2) Management;
3) Making excuses;
4) Blaming others.

Success comes from staying in the creative stage—by continuing to build, not resting on laurels. Those who try to manage others will not succeed in this business because that leads down the path to making excuses and blaming people and circumstances.

An essential key to my own success in this business was a do-or-die attitude. Financial independence and freedom for me and my family was so important that I had to have it in my life or else I was going to die.

I decided never to get discouraged. Disappointed, maybe.

People are not predictable. Sometimes they don't show up for appointments. They cancel at the last minute without thinking to tell you. I just decided to keep going.

Like a honey bee going from flower to flower, I just kept offering myself to people, offering an opportunity, a better way to live. I plugged into a training and support system of books, tapes, seminars, and the leaders in my business Network, and I decided to stay positive and upbeat, no matter what.

I decided to get my goals. It is only a decision. The actual work and effort is ridiculously easy. It's making the decision to do it that is hard.

Major decisions to take control of your life will be met with all types of challenges mainly in the form of other people who choose to remain ignorant, apathetic and lazy. But you can't change other people. You can only work on yourself.

Building your Network Marketing business may be the greatest personal leadership challenge in America. You will have no authority over anyone. You can only set the example with high standards and expectations, and then be the example.

People are dying to know what you know.

This success system works if you work it.

You'll need to build up your attitude with books and tapes.

You'll need to change and grow.

With the right mental attitude and the right financial vehicle, you can convert your dreams into a life.

Remember, the only person you can count on is you.

If it's to be, it's up to me.

Whose dream is it, anyway?

It's yours, and you'll have to make the decision to put forth the effort.

Stay focused. It's not easy—but it's incredibly rewarding. And it's certainly better than being broke.

Nobody said success is easy. They just said, "Many people have done it. You can do it, too."

In the next chapter, you'll learn what it takes to set up your Network Marketing business and organize your home office. It's very simple. It's inexpensive. You don't need very much at all to get started.

CHAPTER 7
Setting Up Your Business

After you have chosen a Network Marketing opportunity, signed your application and become familiar with the materials in your business kit, you are ready to get started. And the first get-started step is to select a name for your business.

Use a simple name with your last name in it, like Smith Enterprises or Jones International. Do not use initials, like IBM. Nobody will know what the initials mean. It took IBM 30 years to create their "initial" name recognition.

When your company name is based on your last name, you don't need to file a *dba*, "doing business as," which is known as a fictitious name. It costs money to file a fictitious business name with your county recorder. Part of the requirements for filing a *dba* is that you publish your *dba* in the newspaper, and that costs money, also.

Avoid paying for a business license. Your independent, home-based Network Marketing business does not need a business license. The business license department in your city reads the published fictitious names. They will send you a bill for a business license if your *dba* is listed there.

Your Network Marketing business starts out small, requiring very little time or money to get started. In the beginning, you are the business. Later, you might want to consider other ways to legally structure your business, but not until it gets larger. You might want to consider incorporating. A corporation may offer additional tax benefits and protection from other liabilities, because it separates you personally from your business.

When your business grows, after a year or two, consult your attorney and your accountant. Explore the advantages and disadvantages of incorporating your business. Ask your sponsor and the leaders of your distributor organization for their ideas also.

You need business cards immediately.

Visit a printer and design a simple, professional business card. Cards are cheap. Order a thousand. Keep it simple. Do not use pictures, designs, logos, descriptions, or clever sayings. Let the printer help you arrange your business name, your name, address and business telephone number on your card. Use high-quality white paper and black ink.

After you have been in business for a year or two, you will have traded business cards with hundreds or thousands of people. You will have seen many different cards, and you might get ideas for improving yours. You will be able to redesign your card every time you need to print more.

Share your card with everyone. Ask other people for their card. If they don't have one, write their name and phone number on the back of one of yours, and add them to your list of prospects when you get home. Include your card in every letter that you send. Staple your card to the brochures and promotional materials that you use.

Do not use rubber stamps and ink pads. The ink smears. A rubber stamp leaves the impression of poverty. It does not create a professional look.

Ask the printer to quote a price for 1000 matching letterhead and envelopes using the same style of printing and paper quality as your business cards. If you can afford the expense, order the business stationery right away, too. When you write letters, you want people to know that you take your business seriously. You will have many opportunities to send short business letters.

Every time you meet a new person, it is a very nice touch to send a letter thanking them for their time, or simply telling them you enjoyed meeting with them. You will find countless reasons to send short notes to people, even for no other reason than to stay in touch, which is the best reason.

Get a separate telephone number and telephone that you use strictly for business.

Answer it professionally. "Hello, this is Sally." Your family shouldn't answer the business line unless you have trained them how to be courteous and respectful and how to take complete messages for you.

Answering the phone professionally means saying your name or your company name clearly, in a friendly way, in an enthusiastic manner that welcomes the caller. Be sure you sit up straight and smile every time you answer the phone or call someone. People know when you are smiling, even though they cannot see you; a smiling voice is a friendly voice, and a friendly voice is an attractive voice.

They also know when you are a slouch; they can hear it. You can't slouch and sound enthusiastic at the same time.

As your business grows, you will receive calls from people whom you may not know very well or not at all, and you want to make a good first impression, a business impression.

Another reason for having a separate telephone number for your business is that you can deduct all of the phone expenses, including the telephone set itself. The entire phone bill is a business expense.

Use an answering machine or an electronic voice mail service on your business line.

Make sure you can easily change your greeting message. Keep your greeting short, simple, and professional. No music, no jokes. Be sure it sounds friendly.

Make sure you can retrieve your messages from another telephone anytime. Be sure your answering system includes the time and date on every message. Make sure your callers have plenty of time to talk; some answering machines cut off your caller after 15 or 20 seconds; that's rude, and you may not get their entire message.

Do not use live answering services. They are impersonal, and they usually will only take a brief message, like a name and number only. Answering machines and voice mail services let the caller leave a detailed message.

Now you have a business name with business cards and stationery and a business telephone. You are in business. All you need are some people to do business with and a few basic tools.

Where should you set up your business?

Make a permanent place in your home where you can run your business. You can start small. Set up a card table, chair and lamp in the corner of a room. Install your business phone there.

Choose a place for your small office that is out of the traffic flow of your home. You'll want some quiet and privacy when you are talking with people on the phone. You'll need good lighting and fresh air. Being able to see out a window is nice. If you have a spare room, dedicate the entire room to your business, and tell your accountant. You might want to make use of the home-office tax deduction which is available if your home-office is your principal place of business and when you do not use the room for any other purpose.

You will need tablets, pencils, pens, a calculator that prints a tape, and an alphabetical 3 x 5 card system next to your phone. Get some simple manila folders and a drawer or a box to keep them in. Label them as you need them for keeping track of orders, back-orders, brochures, tax information and receipts, important letters, etc. Organize a little, so you can find something when you need it. Spend 10 percent of your time staying organized and 90 percent of your time in the creative stage of building your business.

Get some pictures from magazines or brochures of the things you want, your dreams and goals, the rewards that your business can provide. Put those pictures on the wall by your desk or table so you see them every day.

Keep reminding yourself why you are building your business. (Sometimes you just might need reminding!)

The most important item that you will learn to depend on in building your business is a calendar/organizer.

Get a serious one. Look at the various sizes and formats available from Daytimer, Franklin Day Planner® or others. Get one with plenty of room for writing.

You'll need a place to write notes, priorities, phone numbers, and plenty of room to list daily "to-do" items. It's helpful to be able to see a "month at a glance" or a "week at a glance." Make sure you have plenty of room to write several appointments in a day. Buy the best calendar that you can afford. Learn to use it—and keep it with you *always*.

Open a separate checking account for your business. All you need is a second personal checking account. Most banks charge more for business checking accounts, so don't ask for business checks. Just open another personal checking account. Open it with a small amount of money. Have them print your business name, address and phone number on the checks.

Make sure that you use your business checking account for business expenses, and keep your personal checking account separate from the business. Talk to your accountant. Learn to become aware of business expenses. Balance your checkbook often. If you bounce a check twice, you may be put on a permanent cash status.

One of the best reasons to own a business is that you get to deduct business expenses from your income taxes. It is one of the last legal tax shelters.

What is a business expense?

Anything you buy or do in the course of building your business is an expense.

One of the great things about a Network Marketing business is that virtually everyone is a prospect for your business, and virtually every activity can be combined with business.

You are always building your business. Invest some time with your tax expert or accountant and learn how to create and track legitimate business expenses.

Keep a list of all your tax deductible business expenses; entertainment, travel, books, seminars, tapes, parking, bridge tolls, copies, office supplies, office equipment, postage, shipping, phone bills, other utilities, car mileage and repairs, product samples, promotional materials, sales tools, and more.

Baby-sitting is not a business expense. Pay your baby-sitter with your personal check, not cash. You may be able to get a child-care credit on your personal taxes.

Keep a tablet in your car to record your odometer to document business trips. Ask your accountant. You can deduct about 30 cents per mile for business travel.

Paying for business expenses with your checkbook is the best way to keep track of those expenses.

Sometimes you need to pay cash, so save the receipt and write the names of the people you entertained, the date, description of the event, amount, and method of payment on the receipt.

Keep 12 envelopes in an expense file, one for each month. Each day, put your business receipts in this month's envelope. Save all of your receipts this way and give them to your accountant at tax time.

When you use a credit card, save that receipt, also. It is a good idea to use one credit card for business only, separate from personal shopping. At tax time, you will save time by not having to separate the personal charges from the business expenses on the credit card statements.

Do you need a computer?

No.

Even if you already have a computer, run your business manually at first until you know what you are doing. A computer only helps when you already know what you are doing. The software you choose should match your way of doing business. You don't want to change your way of doing business just to conform to some software package that you bought.

Become completely familiar with your business manually before you attempt to automate it.

However, once you do so, you can use the computer for *everything*— your calendar, your list of prospects and business associates, personal mailings to groups of distributors or customers, your accounting, your personal correspondence including faxes, on-line ordering from your supplier, everything. When you do set up your business on a computer, be sure you have a fail-safe backup system for all your data, and be sure to backup daily.

What about a fax machine, a cellular phone, a copier, and a two-line phone?

Buy them if you can afford them when your business volume grows to the point that you think you need them. Don't buy them just so people will think you are successful. It doesn't matter what other people think. You'll know when you need those things.

Become a student of the business. Ask your sponsor how best to handle the details of ordering products. The key to your business is duplication: do the things that are tried and true. Ask what works. Copy the system that successful people already have devised. Run your business *right* from the beginning.

Duplication is profitable.

Innovation will cost you money and time.

All you need now are some people to work with. You know people, and they know people, and all you need to do is go talk to them.

How many people do you know? You're about to find out.

How many people don't you know? That's the exciting part.

The people you know will lead you to the people you don't know, and you will build a large business with people you don't know yet.

Get your tablet out and write a list of people you know. The idea is to list every person that you know. Make no decision as to whether or not they would be interested in talking to you about an exciting business idea. You won't know if they are interested until you show it to them.

Every business starts with a list of prospects. We talked about this earlier, but now let's get really specific. This will be the single most important thing that you do for yourself and teach to the people whom you sponsor into your business Network.

You may not ever get around to calling some of them. You might not want to work with some of them. At this stage, it doesn't matter. Just create a list!

This process of building your list of prospects is *the most critical activity* you will perform in getting your business started.

Gather up all of your Christmas lists, photo albums, church directories, birthday lists, personal telephone directories, high school and college yearbooks, club directories and any other lists that you keep. Write down all of the names and phone numbers of everyone on those lists.

Next, add the names of all other friends, relatives and neighbors.

Next, think about all of the people that you know, whether you know their names or not, whether you feel you really know them or not. People that you see from time to time in your daily travels and errands are people that you know.

Here is a list of people to get you started.

Who is your:
    Milkman . . . ?
    Mail carrier . . . ?
    Paper boy or girl . . . ?
    Dentist . . . ?
    Physician . . . ?
    Nurse . . . ?
    Minister . . . ?
    Florist . . . ?
    Lawyer . . . ?
    Insurance agent . . . ?
    Accountant . . . ?
    Congressperson . . . ?
    Pharmacist . . . ?

Veterinarian . . . ?
Optometrist . . . ?

Who sold you your:
House . . . ?
Car . . . ?
Tires . . . ?
Piano . . . ?
Fishing tackle . . . ?
Television . . . ?
Stereo . . . ?
Suit . . . ?
Shoes . . . ?
Business cards . . . ?
Office supplies . . . ?
Wedding rings . . . ?
Glasses or contacts . . . ?
Vacuum cleaner . . . ?
Boat . . . ?
Camper . . . ?
Bicycle . . . ?
Living room furniture . . . ?
Kitchen appliances . . . ?
Lawnmower . . . ?
Luggage . . . ?
Carpet . . . ?
Coffee maker . . . ?

Who lives next door . . . ?
Who lives across the street . . . ?
Who are your babysitter's parents . . . ?
Who teaches at school . . . ?
Who was your best man . . . ?
Who were the ushers and bridesmaids . . . ?

Who was your maid of honor ...?

Who was the photographer ...?

Who is the purchasing agent at work ...?

Who goes fishing ...?

Who goes hunting ...?

Who was an army buddy ...?

Who was your architect ...?

Who goes bowling ...?

Who is active in the PTA ...?

Who was in college with you ...?

Who goes camping ...?

Who do you work with ...?

Who is the manager at the store ...?

Who is your boss ...?

Who is your former boss ...?

Who repaired your TV ...?

Who upholstered your couch ...?

Who did you work with at your former job ...?

Who goes to the races ...?

Who is in your car pool ...?

Who installed your telephone ...?

Who owns a laundromat ...?

Who teaches ceramics ...?

Who drives a taxi ...?

Who is your gardener ...?

Who painted your house ...?

Who owns the pet shop ...?

Who installed your refrigerator ...?

Who renewed your driver's license ...?

Who manages apartments ...?

Who is active in Lions, Rotary or Optimists clubs ...?

Who is in a garden club ...?

Who teaches kindergarten ...?

Who is a deacon at church ...?

Who are the parents of your children's friends ... ?
Who owns a drapery business ... ?
Who gave you a speeding ticket ... ?
Who does your income tax ... ?
Who works at the drycleaners ... ?
Who hangs wallpaper ... ?
Who teaches driver's education ... ?
Who is a paramedic ... ?
Who owns the resort where you took a vacation ... ?
Who sells gasoline ... ?
Who repairs your car ... ?
Who sells wigs ... ?
Who owns a nursery ... ?
Who drives a UPS truck ... ?
Who has a pest exterminator business ... ?
Who sells ice cream ... ?
Who sells jewelry ... ?
Who sells aluminum awnings ... ?
Who works at the travel agency ... ?

Who is ...

A nurse ... ?
Golf pro ... ?
Student ... ?
Fashion model ... ?
Security guard ... ?
Sheriff ... ?
Fire chief ... ?
Truck driver ... ?
Secretary ... ?
Welder ... ?
Crane operator ... ?
Candy salesperson ... ?
Music teacher ... ?

Art teacher ... ?
Forester ... ?
Seamstress ... ?
Carpenter ... ?
Pilot ... ?
Flight attendant ... ?
Editor ... ?
Lab technician ... ?
Restaurant owner ... ?
Social worker ... ?
Race car driver ... ?
Paper mill worker ... ?
Brick mason ... ?
Drafting manager ... ?
Printer ... ?
Office manager ... ?
Bakery owner ... ?
Plant foreman ... ?
Anesthetist ... ?
Surgeon ... ?
Librarian ... ?
Mortician ... ?
Real estate agent ... ?
Railroad engineer ... ?
Newspaper pressman ... ?
Bulldozer operator ... ?
Mobile home salesperson ... ?
Airline ticket agent ... ?
Computer programmer ... ?
Motor home dealer ... ?
Soft drink distributor ... ?
Air traffic controller ... ?
Lifeguard ... ?
Swimming teacher ... ?

Interior decorator ... ?

Computer salesperson ... ?

Grocery store owner ... ?

Insurance adjuster ... ?

Music store manager ... ?

Escrow officer ... ?

College instructor ... ?

Literary agent ... ?

Anyone and everyone else ... ?

I think you get the idea. The world—*your* world—is full of people of all types, roles and occupations. Which ones are most likely to be interested in what you have to offer? You simply don't know—you can't know. Not until you ask; and you probably won't ask until you put them on your list.

Next, if your Network Marketing supplier publishes a magazine in which they recognize achievers with photographs and names, get into the habit of reading the names and occupations, because a face or a name or occupation can jog your memory and help you think of someone to add to your prospect list.

You don't have to "know" someone to *know them*. It's enough that you recognize them, or that they would recognize or remember you, even vaguely, and you can introduce yourself and talk to them.

You can add to your list of prospects daily because you meet new people every day. Start saying "Hi" to people, and smile. Just practice. When you have the opportunity, practice using F.O.R.M. (Family, Occupation, Recreation, Marketing Message) and just be a friend. Ask people for business cards, and offer your card, and you will continually build your list.

Once you have your list, whom do you call first?

Start with those closest to home. Pick the most successful people, and go see them first. Identify those who are leaders, those who have influence with other people. Choose those who are outgoing and upbeat, positive people who like people and who like being around people.

Once again, this is a people business, not a product business. When you organize people in a Network Marketing business, the products and services will naturally flow through the Network.

How do you get an appointment?

Pick up the phone, dial the number, and ask if you can come over to drop off some information about an exciting business idea. Tell them you are in a hurry, and that you can't stay.

When they ask, "What is it?" ask them in return, "Are you interested in other ways of making money?" Almost everyone will answer "Yes" to that question. If someone says no, they are not a prospect, so call someone else.

Use the telephone to get appointments. Be friendly and relaxed, not pushy or hyped. Be yourself. Do not try to explain something over the phone; it's too difficult. Tell people that. Say:

I can't explain it over the phone, but I can drop off some information if you are interested in other ways of making money.

I'm involved in a wholesale/retail business where we save money and show other people how to do the same thing. Are you open to other ways of making money, or are you pretty much committed to your job for the rest of your life?

Loan them this book or a tape or a brochure and set a definite time within 48 hours to come back and pick it up. Be sure to keep your appointment. I don't call to confirm my follow-up appointments, because many times fear sets in and the prospect cancels or postpones the meeting.

When you return to pick up the information that you loaned them, ask what they liked best about it. Whatever they say, offer to give them more information. If they are interested, take 45 minutes and enthusiastically show them the example in this book of how anyone can make an extra $2000 a month in Network Marketing, part-time. Explain that it is a conservative example, not a promise.

When they understand the idea of Network Marketing, then specifically show them your own business opportunity. Introduce your compensation plan, your supplier and the products and services. Leave more information, and set an exact time to come back and pick up the materials within 48 hours.

When you come back, they will have questions and objections. Learn to answer questions and objections clearly. You will hear the same ones over and over with variations on the basic themes. Ask your sponsor how to answer the most common questions and objections.

Show them how they can get started now with very little time or money, and make sure they understand that you will help them and that there is an active distributor organization and a proven, Eight-Step Success System. They can't fail. (Unless they never try.)

Most people will want the business, but they will not have confidence in themselves, and they won't believe that they can do it. So, they will often say they don't have the money to get started, or that they don't have the time.

You can already answer both of those objections, or excuses, just by having read this far in this book. Both responses are cries for help based on low self-esteem and lack of priorities. Use the Feel, Felt, Found formula. Be sincere.

Learn how to answer the questions. There aren't very many different ones. Ask your sponsor. Take your sponsor or active upline with you on your appointments. Your business will take off faster, and you will learn faster. Ask for help. Remember, your sponsor has a personal and financial interest in your success.

Many of the people on your list are excellent prospects who may not know you over the phone, or you may not have their name and phone number. For those, go see them in person as you run your errands and travel around town.

Prospect as you go.

Don't "go prospecting."

Don't "go hunting" for people.

Just do what you normally do—and prospect as you go.

Have copies of books or tapes and business cards with you all the time. Be prepared to share your business when the opportunity arises. Keep your calendar with you—*always!*

Be willing to learn the business from people who are successful.

Learn to do the right things over and over.

Develop creative enthusiasm.

Treat your business like a big business from the beginning.

Invest five solid years in building your business, part-time, and it will take care of you full-time for the rest of your life—and it'll take care of your heirs beyond that, too.

Sponsor as many people as possible in your personal business width in the first two years. Work with a few who really want to work.

Build your business depth through the people you sponsor. Find out who they know, and help them to make a list, and help them explain the business concept to their prospects. Go with them on their appointments.

Build your depth by working with three or four groups at a time. When you sponsor someone, help her sponsor three people. Pick the most ambitious of these three and help that person sponsor three, and on and on, and keep building depth downline in that leg of sponsorship, until you are working in depth at least ten deep.

Learn to do the creative basics of the business, and do them over and over and over. The basics consist of showing the business to new people and ordering products on a regular basis.

This is not the convincing business. It is the sorting business.

You are just looking for people who are sick and tired of being sick and tired. They're stuck financially and are looking for a way to keep growing.

You are just looking for the people who want to create a better life, and you identify them by showing them the Network Marketing business idea.

There is no other way to know whether someone will join your business. That is why you have to talk to everyone, one at a time, to find out if they qualify.

Setting a good example is a key to success.

Work is the best therapy in the world

People are drawn to your enthusiasm.

When you talk to new people on your list, make a 3 x 5 card for them with their name, address, phone number, and a brief note about your visit, including the date. Keep your cards in alphabetical order, and every time you call someone or talk to someone, make a brief note on their card, so you can remember what you talked about.

You'll talk to a lot of people in your business. You don't want to try to remember everything about everyone. Use your cards to help your memory.

Get people's birthdays and send them birthday cards.

Get their children's names and their pets' names.

Get to know the people in your business.

The purpose of any meeting is to share more information and enthusiasm *and* to set another meeting in your calendar.

Stop majoring in survival. Change your major and start living.

You can do a lot more with money than without it.

You can help more people when you have money.

Nobody ever said money was evil; they said the *love of money* was bad.

Love people and use money. Not the other way around.

Keep your answers short. Don't explain your explanation.

Forget worrying about doing things right.

Do the right things, even if you do them wrong at first.

Duplicate your time, energy and knowledge through others, and your rewards will be automatic.

Inspire, encourage and teach.

Draw out other people's desires for a better life, for their own success.

Work with those who are willing to work. Spend 80 percent of your time with 20 percent of the people in your group. They are the leaders.

Delegation is communication.

Stay away from people who are looking for a handout. You can't give someone success, but you can help them get it themselves. Give people a hand up, not a handout.

Put a value on your time. Whether you have three people in your business, or 3000, they will take all of your time if you let them. Leverage your time instead. It's not how much time you have, it's how you invest it that matters.

Give your leaders an assignment, and tell them to call back when they've finished.

Give them an appointment for more training and for another assignment.

Remember, you're the coach and the cheerleader.

Three Kinds of Meetings

I have three types of regular meetings with the ambitious associates in my Network Marketing business.

The first meeting is a presentation of the Network Marketing idea.

I make this one-hour presentation to new distributors and prospects. It's a condensed outline of the first five chapters of this book. I make this presentation three to four times a week, usually in the evening in the home of one of the distributors in my Network.

The second type of meeting is a detailed presentation of the Eight-Step Success System I described in chapter six.

This is a mini-seminar for distributors, a short course in how to build a successful Network Marketing business in the quickest possible way. I try to hold one of these meetings once a week in a distributor's home.

The third type of meeting is an "Attitude and Principles" session.

These happen once a month in the home of one of the distributors in my Network. I talk about a book I'm currently reading or a tape set that I'm studying, and these are usually titles from the recommended list of books and tapes at the back of this book.

This is a great way to create interest in books and tapes. Everyone gets a chance to share experiences and ask questions. At these meetings, we share our weekly and monthly goals for building our businesses, and we challenge each other and create an environment of accountability for achieving the goals that we give ourselves. We recognize each other's accomplishments and provide encouragement to overcome the obstacles that we all have to deal with to succeed.

In each of these three types of meetings, the groups grow in size, and eventually other distributors in my group take the lead and start to hold their own meetings, duplicating a successful, proven system.

These meetings create lasting personal relationships with business associates in the Network. They foster integrity and honesty.

These meetings form the basis of leadership, training and recognition, and they help build the positive relationships, which keep us all motivated, interested and productive—and honest with each other.

The associations that develop from these nightly, weekly and monthly meetings create a powerful sense of teamwork. We have fun, and we know we are building our futures together, which is very satisfying.

I make sure to attend every seminar or rally where a successful leader in the business is teaching. I take notes and record the seminar. I also encourage everyone in my business Network to be there.

Being around people who are already successful in the same business is one of the smartest things you can do to get your own business up and running quickly. Learn from those who are where you want to be in the business. I stay after the seminar and meet the speakers.

Practice, practice, practice doing the basic things that work.
Practice makes up for your lack of skill in the beginning.
Practice makes permanent.
Massive action gets your business going.

Teach people to teach others to teach. Set high, realistic goals, and measure your results. Maintain high personal values of honesty and integrity. Consistence and persistence are keys. Care more about long-term results than about short-term profits.

Patience and endurance are a winning combination.
A positive attitude is your best asset.
Your attitude determines your altitude.

If you are not making mistakes, you are not growing. Learn from mistakes, adjust your course, reset your goals.

Don't spend time reviving people. People who buy a business kit but never go talk to anyone will always fail to build a business. It's easier and more fun to run with a hundred than to try to drag one.

People are setting goals and getting back to work at the beginning of the year when they set their New Year's resolutions.

At the end of summer when school starts, people are getting back to their routines.

What is the best time to build your Networking business?

The next six months are the best months, no matter what time of year it is!

Get to the top by helping other people up. The money comes automatically when you help other people get what they want.

Motivation is inside out.
Get hold of a dream that gets you fired up.
The sooner you start, the easier it will be to finish.
Get going and get it over with.
Build your business fast.
Surround yourself with successful people.
Keep working.

You reap what you sow, but you never harvest in the same season that you plant.

Begin right where you are now. You don't need to do anything else first.

We have a three-foot rule: A prospect is anyone within three feet of you. You start the conversation, trade cards, ask questions but don't interrogate. Tell them what you do in a way that has something in it for them. Loan them a book or tape. Get an appointment.

If you don't have anything to loan them right then, call them the next day and ask for an appointment to share some information about your business.

Anyone can become an expert in this business.

Anybody can become successful if they just follow the system. The system has been designed to guarantee unlimited expansion for the person willing to work the system.

Your success will depend on your ability to instill vision and self-esteem in people.

Teach independence and self-confidence, not dependence and doubt.

The people you sponsor will duplicate what you do, but they'll probably only do about half as much as you do.

People are power.

Do the right things.

Build trust.

Build a culture of achievement.

Express a vision.

Build team players.

Keep your promises.

Help people win.

Success attracts success. Act the part. Believe in yourself.

Develop success consciousness.

Learn to leverage time and money. That's the key.

CHAPTER 8
Time and Money

"All my possessions for a moment of time."
—Queen Elizabeth I, with her dying breath, 1603

Time and leisure are to the 90s what money was to the 80s.
Time is hard to buy.
Time has become the most precious commodity in the land.
Time is the currency of the 90s and 21st Century.
Time freedom is not the same as money. It is more valuable.

Why do we work so hard and have so little time?
Most people never get control of time and money.
Most people spend all their time chasing money.

Your income is whatever it is, and expenses have a way of rising to meet and exceed your income. We always want more, and many of us financed the extras with plastic. Credit cards came in the mail. It's common now for people to carry six or seven credit cards with them.

When you sit down at the beginning of the month to pay the bills, it's too tempting to just pay the minimum payment amount, and you get buried in debt that way. You become a slave to the lender. Pretty soon you're making interest payments on things you don't even have anymore.

You know you're in financial trouble when you catch yourself wishing that you could just get back to simply being broke again.

Most families are about $400 short at the end of every month.

In the 1940s and 1950s, the typical single-income family paid 15 to 20 percent of their income for taxes and housing.

In the 1980s and 1990s, taxes and housing consumed 70 to 75 percent of the income of the typical dual-income family.

In the 1980s, inflation wiped out the wage gains of the majority of working people. There isn't any money left for the savings account today.

If you save as much money in the next five years as you saved in the past five years, will you be excited?

You need to save money for emergencies and future expenditures, but it's not possible to save your way to success. That implies an attitude of lack, of cutting back and scarcity—an attitude that leads to failure.

In the 80s, many Americans came to worship career status as a measure of personal worth. Many were willing to sacrifice any amount of leisure time to get ahead. Work became trendy. The 80-hour week was a status symbol.

No more.

For many exhausted American families in the 90s, the high value of free time is affecting their philosophy of materialism and their career considerations. There's a new rebellion against the rat race, against the establishment. The new status for mothers is to be able to afford to stay home and be full-time Moms—even with less income.

The irony is that time is only a notion.

Time cannot be physically captured and examined. Scientists don't talk about time; it doesn't actually exist. They refer to the time-space continuum, whatever that is. Nature respects only the rhythm of the universe.

The idea of time itself exists only in your mind.

People invented the idea of time and then created clocks to measure it. As a human invention, time exists purely in relation to your perception of it. But in the vast universe, what is an hour or a minute? What if you could live your life not as a slave to time but within the natural rhythm of the universe?

Time expands and contracts. It is not certain.

What about those times when you are fully absorbed in a project that you love, and you lose all sense of time, and the hours fly by, but it seems like minutes?

How about other times when you are waiting or agonizing, anxiously, and time is standing still, and the thing you are waiting for takes forever?

Time can be so-o-o-o slow.

Learn the difference between the urgent things and the important things.

Urgent things demand your time but can usually wait, even when they seem like emergencies.

Important things move you in the direction of your dreams and goals, and this is where you need to focus your time.

It is not possible to manage time. But you can make more time by leveraging it. It is your most precious commodity, your only natural resource.

You can have more time by changing the way you relate to the idea of time.

You can live in a world of scarcity or abundance.

You can manage your priorities, but you cannot manage time.

It is the same with money.

You don't manage money; you manage your priorities.

You can live in a world of abundance or in a world of scarcity.

You choose your world by choosing your thoughts. Thoughts are causes, and your life is an effect.

Money comes from serving people, from investing time in other people.

When you leverage time and serve more people, more money comes to you.

When you focus on helping others and forget about yourself, money pours into your life.

When you focus on your own needs and count your money, you are focused on lack—lack of money, lack of things you want, and that is what you create.

You become what you think about. Think about serving people, the money will take care of itself.

Financial hardship is self-inflicted.

It comes from thinking only of yourself.

Financial problems are the easiest kind of problems to cure. Take your eyes off yourself and focus on the needs and wants of others, and unselfishly help other people. When you help enough other people to get what they want, you can have anything you want.

Money is simply the yardstick of service rendered. It is a tool, a medium of exchange, a reward for creating volume. You are paid for your contribution to volume, no matter what you do for a living.

When you focus on problems, you will always have more problems. You create whatever you focus on. Solve one problem, and your mind gives you another one. If you look for negative, you will find it. That is why spending time solving problems is not productive.

You always find what you are looking for. In the high desert, the buzzard circles, looking for decaying flesh—and he finds it. In the same sky, the hummingbird is focused on the sweet nectar of brilliant flowers blooming in the cactus, in the same desert—and she finds it.

Own your future, focusing on what you want, leveraging your time in activities that advance you directly toward definite dreams and goals. It's your future.

Procrastination is the thief of time and the graveyard of opportunity.

If you wait until you have time, you'll be waiting forever. You will never have time. It's the most elusive concept ever devised. That's why there's no such thing as tomorrow.

Try to find a calendar with a tomorrow on it.

There's only today.

Tomorrow is a promissory note. Yesterday is a canceled check. Do it now!

When your priorities are in order, you know what you need to do right now. Just do it. Think in terms of cracks of time. Grab those little bits of time and do a little bit at a time toward your goal. You'll soon find those cracks widening, expanding, because you are focused on having time.

Only dead people don't have time. They're also the only ones with no problems. It's not a matter of having time, but of arranging your priorities.

I order my priorities in life in the following order:

1) Spiritual—My God
2) Family—My most treasured possession
3) Country—My patriotic duty
4) Job—My primary income
5) Business—My Network Marketing business

When I consider these priorities while making decisions about how to allocate time and energy, I keep my life in order, in perspective. If there is a question about which is more important, a business appointment or a family event, it's clear, the family takes priority. My life has a sense of order and purpose, a sense of balance.

You always have time.

You make time.

You have all the time there is.

You have the same 24 hours as everybody else.

Time is already right here, right now.

You make time for the things you want to do.

Here are some results from a very interesting Gallup Poll:

- 80 percent of Americans say time moves too fast for them.
- 54 percent say they feel under pressure to get everything done.
- 51 percent say they don't have time to the things they want to do.

People say they are busy. Being too busy comes from focusing on the urgent things, the little emergencies that always seem to pop up. When your priorities are clear, you focus on your goals and attend to the important things, and the urgent things will go away.

Work is the common denominator robbing most people of their time.

Most people would rather work four days, not five days a week, but they can't afford that.

Most people are under time pressure, because they spend all their time chasing money.

If you are trading time for dollars, you are spending all your time.

When you spend all your time, you become time bankrupt. To create more time, you need to invest little cracks of time in other people.

Duplicate yourself.

Leverage your time.

Some more fascinating results, this time from a Time/CNN Poll:

- 60 percent of all Americans want to slow down and live a more relaxed life.
- 61 percent said earning a living today requires so much effort that it's difficult to find time to enjoy life.
- 89 percent said it was more important to have time with their families.
- 56 percent felt strongly about needing time for personal interests and hobbies.
- Only seven percent thought it was important to shop for status symbols.

What would most people do with more time? They want to:

- have more time with families or friends;
- relax and rest;
- travel and see the world.

Instead of defining themselves primarily by their possessions and their work, more Americans are finding meaningful identify and purpose by getting involved in their communities and helping people. People want more time around hearth and home. Do you?

Focus on your priorities.

Stop struggling to keep up with the people who seem to be making it big. They are probably deeply in debt and struggling to get out of it. Be your own leader by knowing what you want.

Comparison leads to failure. Conformity will keep you broke.

Multiple incomes (not dual incomes) are the wave of the future. Learn to leverage time and diversify your income. Invest time in other people. Duplicate your time and energy through other people. Get out from under the control of time and money. You be in control.

When your Network Marketing business is producing residual income, you will find yourself with plenty of money and plenty of time, and you can stop worrying about money and start living.

When you learn to take away the time pressure, you realize that *you* were creating the pressure.

Time doesn't care.

The universe doesn't care.

You create your own pressure when your sense of values and priorities is unclear.

Without that self-inflicted pressure and tension, you can start thinking long-term. Successful people think long-term. They plan tomorrow and next week, but they also visualize next year and five years from now and 20 years from now.

Short-term thinking will keep you broke.

Develop your own mental pictures for how you want to live, own your future by imagining it, and hold that picture long-term.

Your thoughts are like the Chinese bamboo.

One day a little sprig pops out of the ground, but it doesn't seem to grow. In fact, all you see for *four years* is this little sprig just poking above the ground while it sends its roots deep, deep into the soil. Then, one day, when it knows it has a root foundation to support itself, it begins to grow fast—and it shoots up 90 feet in six weeks.

That's long-term thinking. Sacrifice a little bit of what you want today to be able to have a lot of what you want in the future.

That's how a Network Marketing business grows.

It seems like nothing is happening while you whittle away at it in little cracks of time, investing a bit of time here and some more over there, and for two to five years you drive the roots of your business very deep. And sometimes you can't tell that anything is happening. Then, when *it's* ready, it shoots up—and your rewards are the fruit on the tree, and with those deep roots, your business has a foundation that will support you and your family *permanently.*

CHAPTER 9
Success, Dreams and Goals

Success is different for everyone.

Success is the path along which you travel, learn, and grow in the pursuit of what you want. It is the progressive realization of your worthwhile dreams and goals.

Success is getting and doing more of the things you want.

Success is having peace of mind.

Success is having both time and money.

Success comes from serving people and creating an unlimited volume of products and services.

Success is the result of leveraging your time.

Success is never convenient.

Success is always a risk. That's the key.

If you want to have more tomorrow than you have today, then you'll have to risk doing things differently today than you did yesterday.

When you do things differently, you operate outside your comfort zone. Get used to it.

Don't worry about your fears and doubts. They're normal.

Don't sweat the small stuff. And, know that it's all small stuff.

What is Required for Success?

1) Written goals—and a burning desire for what you want.
2) Positive mental attitude, an open mind and people skills.
3) Determination, action and hard work.
4) Delayed gratification and long-term thinking.
5) Willingness to duplicate a proven system.
6) Willingness to imitate the habits of successful people.
7) The sincere desire to serve others and to help them get what they want.
8) 100 percent commitment, persistence and consistent effort.
9) A no-limit, high-leverage financial vehicle.
10) A friendly alliance with one or more persons who will encourage you.

You need to forget your past failures. Learn from them—then get rid of them. Failure is just an event, an outcome, a learning experience, a stepping stone to success. Successful people have experienced many failures. For them, failures are only past events. Water under the bridge.

You are not a failure.

You are not the event.

You are a winner!

If you want to double your success rate, then double your failure rate. Focus on your future, not on your past.

You need to keep your mind closely guarded against all negative and discouraging influences, including the negative suggestions of relatives, friends and acquaintances.

Replace the negative effects of other people and the media with the positive influence of your dream. Keep your dream in focus, in front of you all the time. Put pictures of what you want—spiritual or material things—in places where you will see them first thing in the morning, during the day, and the last thing at night before you go to bed.

Success for many people began with a self-improvement book or tape, and that started a lifelong learning program. Successful people study success principles. The books and tapes are available. The information is not secret, but you have to get it and apply it.

It is a lot easier to talk about success than to apply the proven principles of success.

The ABCs of Success

ATTITUDE: You can accomplish virtually anything when you think you can. Success is 98 percent positive attitude. You will always get what you expect to get.

BELIEF: When you have faith in yourself and believe in your goals, all kinds of unforeseen circumstances and people will come to your aid.

COMMITMENT: Total commitment = total freedom. When you are committed to your purpose, your integrity, and your values, your goals take on a sense of urgency in your life, and other people start to share your belief.

Your success will be 90 percent why *and 10 percent* how.

Energy comes from wanting something. That's the reason you're reading a book about building a Network Marketing business—you want something, right?

Knowing *why* you are doing something provides permanent, internal motivation. When you want something badly, you don't think about being tired. You get moving and you keep going until you get it. You don't think about how difficult it is.

Knowing *how* is insignificant by comparison.

I could teach a fifth grader how to build a Network Marketing business. She might not have a reason to do it, but she would know how. But what will happen when things become difficult? Will she rise to the challenge? Only if she knows *why*.

So, what do you want?

Why would you be willing to get out of your comfort zone, be uncomfortable for a while, and suffer delayed gratification?

Why would you be willing to spend two to five years building a business?

What would motivate you to get away from the television, get out of the house, and do something about your future?

Your reason *why* will be different from everyone else's reasons. We all have different reasons.

Your reason must be crystal clear to you.

There are two forms of motivation:

ONE: When you want to get *away* from something you don't like. It might be a negative boss, or work situation, or financial situation—anything that you want to move away from.

TWO: When you want to move *toward* something that you want. It might be a positive financial situation or relationship or material reward.

Usually, the two go together. You might want to get away from a negative job situation and go toward a positive financial situation and own your own no-limit business.

If some unforeseen tragedy prevented you from working, how long could you last financially?

Highly specialized professionals know that a health problem or accident would prevent them from working.

The sales professional mysteriously loses her voice and can't work.

The commercial pilot gets a flake of metal in his eye from brushing the dust off the screen door and can't fly.

The dentist breaks her finger in a freak accident and can't work.

The TV store owner goes in the hospital for a liver transplant and can't work for months.

It can happen to you. It does happen—all too often.

Most people would have their television sets repossessed after three months of not having the income to make the payments.

Most people would lose their car after six months of no work.

Most people would lose their house after twelve months of no job.

Most people would be bankrupt in 18 months.

How secure is your income?

Would your income keep coming if you couldn't put in the effort and the hours? How much residual income do you have?

What are you doing about your future?

Where will you be, financially, in two to five years?

Take a look at these statistics:

- Less than one percent of all Americans earn a six-figure income.
- Less than six percent of all Americans earn over $40,000 a year.
- Most people are earning two percent less today than when they started working because of the effects of taxes and inflation in real dollars.
- The average American today has cash assets of only $250 at retirement.
- 12 percent of all people aged 65 and older live in poverty.
- Only five percent of Americans over the age of 65 are financially independent.

On a brighter note, every 12 minutes someone in America becomes a millionaire. There are now over a million and a half millionaires in this country, and many of them made their fortunes in the last 20 years in their own independent, no-limit, high-leverage Network Marketing businesses.

Who are they?

What do they have in common?

They are people just like you and me. They had a burning desire for something more in life; they recognized an opportunity when the door opened and they decided to make the best of it.

They decided to make a difference in their lives.

They decided what they wanted.

They *made it happen.*

98 percent of all Americans don't even know what they want!

They don't think about it. They just survive, going through life just getting by, day to day, paycheck to paycheck.

Stop anyone on the street and ask them, "What is your current major goal?" You'll get a lot of blank stares.

Simply knowing what you want puts you immediately into the top two percent of people in the world. Knowing what you want and having a plan and the right financial vehicle guarantees that you will get it. Take hold of an opportunity!

You need goals.

They are the reasons *why* you will put forth the effort persistently and consistently. Those without goals are doomed to work for those who have goals. Whether you set high goals or low goals, positive or negative goals, you will achieve them.

This book is about dreaming big dreams and setting big goals and wanting them so badly it becomes an empowering emotion.

Most people never set goals because they think they don't have any way to achieve them—so, what's the use? They figure they're just fooling themselves, dreaming up things they want that they don't have any way to ever get.

That thinking is exactly backwards.

First comes the *why,* then comes the *how.*

Harvard University conducted a study which compared their alumni's goals and success.

Of those surveyed:

83 percent had no goals,
14 percent had goals but didn't write them down, and . . .
Three percent had specific written goals.

The study revealed that the group with goals earned three times the income of the group with no goals!

The group with specific, written goals earned 10 times more than the group with no goals!

When you write down what you want, you are on your way to achieving it.

A major advertising agency conducted a national poll. It asked, "If you could have your dream job, what would it be?"

The most popular choice among men was to own and manage their own business, followed by professional athlete, head of a large corporation, forest ranger, and test pilot.

The women's first choice was also to own and manage their own business, followed by tour guide, flight attendant, novelist, and photographer.

Running your own business means you are in control of your future.

We use our powerful brains for little jobs. You decide to buy a new television or take a weekend trip, and you do it. No problem.

But you could just as easily decide to use the same process for bigger things, like creating a new and better way to live.

It's just a matter of thinking bigger.

When you know exactly what you want, you'll have it.

When you know precisely where you want to go, you'll get there.

If you never decide what you want, you'll drift around.

You are the ship's captain.

When you leave port, you know exactly your next destination. You can't see it, but you have a plan for getting there, and you keep the ship moving in the right direction, correcting your course many times on the way, until you reach your destination, no matter how long it takes nor what obstacles come your way.

But what if you left the port and let the ship drift, let the rudder flop around? You could wish, want and hope that the ship would somehow drift all by itself into another port, but it won't. Without a clear destination, a plan *and* a firm hand on the rudder to make course corrections, a storm will smash your ship up on the beach and wreck your future.

Most people think planning means deciding what to do in the future.

What planning really means is deciding what to do today so you'll *have* a future.

It isn't so much a matter of paying the price, or even doing whatever it takes. Achieving goals depends more on you deciding what you are willing to give up to make time for your priorities, to have the time to create your future.

For most people, this means giving up television, that wasted block of time every evening and most of the weekend. Watching commercial television doesn't help you create your future. There is no return on that investment of time. TV dumps negative attitudes and beliefs into your subconscious mind, most of which you wouldn't consciously choose to accept, but you let people whom you don't even know influence your subconscious mind with their negative ideas and behavior.

You might think you are not susceptible, but the programming is getting into your head, and it stays in there, and it affects you.

It is the same thing with the lyrics in the music you listen to. What are they saying? How is it affecting your attitude?

If you listen to sad music where they are singing about how bad they feel and what a rotten life they have and how it just ain't fair—that garbage seeps into your subconscious mind and you absorb it, adopt it and become it.

It's very simple: You are either building your own dream or building someone else's dream. When you watch TV, when you listen to music, whose dream are you building? Yours, or theirs?

It's your choice.

Delayed gratification means not buying things today so you can buy bigger and better things tomorrow.

It means putting off short-term pleasure for long-term happiness.

It means focusing on the goal-achieving activities instead of the stress-relieving activities.

It means saving money and paying off debt today, so you can live a debt-free life with financial security later.

It means focusing on the prize—not the price.

Getting A Life is a process that starts in your imagination. Just like getting the idea for a new television or a weekend trip, you can get a picture in your mind of your future. Then you create some mental pictures of yourself doing certain things in certain ways to make that future happen. You do this all the time. Mostly for little things. Mostly by accident.

Start to use this process for the really big things that can change your life. Just get a picture and a plan.

Your outer world mirrors your inner world. The life you have today is a reflection of the thoughts you had yesterday. You can mentally practice living the life you want. *Get A Life!* is simply a mental rehearsal—the coming attraction of the life you want.

We are all alike in many more ways than we are different. We all want pretty much the same things in life. Psychologists tell us that we all want the same 20 essential things. It's just our priorities about those things that vary.

What do you want most?

If you are like the majority of people, number one is peace of mind. That's the highest goal. The other things on the list help create a quality life that can give us peace of mind.

The Twenty Things We All Want

1) Peace of mind.
2) Own a business (control of financial future, tax benefits).
3) More time with family, good family relationships.
4) Meaningful work with a sense of accomplishment.
5) More time for hobbies and recreation.
6) More friends, deeper relationships, acceptance.
7) Excellent health.
8) Recognition for achievement.
9) Happiness, opportunities for having fun.
10) Education for self and children without financial strain.
11) Be able to contribute generously to charities.

12) First class travel, no more vacations on the relative route.
13) Financial security and no debt.
14) Be able to support family members financially.
15) Nicer house.
16) Nicer car.
17) Prosperity, financial independence.
18) Be able to buy luxuries and material possessions.
19) Not having to worry about unexpected expenses.
20) To leave an estate to heirs.

A Gallup poll shows 62 percent of Americans between age 18 and 29 believe they will be rich someday, yet only nine percent of those 50 and older believe that.

Why?

People quit dreaming as they get older. They give up.

Have you?

To get all the things you want in life, you must increase your income circle. You must overwhelm it with cash flow.

It's a *big* mistake to cut back on your expectations and to give up on getting the things you want. Most people do have it backwards. They're waiting for the income before they decide on their dreams and goals.

You must learn to master the process of dreaming and setting goals first, in order to create your future. (Dreaming and setting goals is part of *Getting A Life.*) Then—with belief and faith—the right financial vehicle for achieving those goals will take you where you want to go. Without a destination, you have no need for a financial vehicle. That's why knowing *why* is more important than knowing *how.*

The last chapter of this book contains a list of recommended books and tapes, and many of them cover the importance of setting goals and the steps for doing it right. I cannot improve on all that is in those books in this short book. But I'll get you started.

You have the right financial vehicle in your grasp. Network Marketing is the most advanced business idea in the business world today, yet it is so simple that anyone can do it.

Get A Life! is a manual for how to put the concept to work for you. But you must know *why* before it will do any good to know *how*.

In Chapter Six, you learned the Eight-Step Success System. When you follow that system, one step at a time, you will build a large, profitable, international, Network Marketing business.

The Eight-Step Success System works. The suppliers are out there and they work, too. The rest is up to you. Work on yourself. Get better.

Would you like to have friends all over the world?

Would you like to be able to travel the world on business trips? People are doing it. So can you.

Would you rather have your income based on one percent of the efforts of a hundred other people, *or* on 100 percent of your own efforts?

Take the one percent. That will give you both time and money.

You can *own your future* as big as you can dream by leveraging your time with your own Network Marketing business.

Take some time to decide specifically what you want from your business. It's the 90 percent of your success. Get very clear, think big. Then, learn to set goals and become accountable to yourself.

Learn to like yourself the way you are; see yourself as whom you will become.

When your dreams and goals are big enough, the obstacles that come your way won't matter, because you'll be focused on what you want.

Most people focus on the things they don't want. That's called worry, and it is a form of negative of goal-setting.

Please understand, your mind cannot focus on the reverse of an idea. When you focus on what you don't want, that's what you'll get.

Fear and doubt cause worry. Worry is the result of indecision.

Anyone can learn to overcome fear and doubt.

You overcome fear by getting into action, by doing the Eight Steps.

You overcome fear with persistence and consistent effort.

And when you do, it does amazing things for your confidence and self-esteem.

Just knowing you are doing something to secure your future makes you feel good. You don't even have to do it well at first. It can be very badly done at first. If you keep going and never quit, you will start producing the results that you want, and you will get your goal.

The Four Basic Principles of Goal Setting

1) The goals must be your own.

2) Your goals must be written down, in the present tense as if already attained, stated in positive language, and constantly held in your mind.

3) You goals must be specific and detailed, achievable and believable.

4) You goals must be measurable with deadlines for their achievement, so you can anticipate their attainment.

Six Areas of Your Life That Benefit From Goal Setting

1) Spiritual
2) Family
3) Social
4) Mental
5) Physical
6) Financial

Set goals in each and every area. Lasting success is a balanced success in all six areas of your life.

When you learn to set goals regularly, you will be less vulnerable to the winds of change that blow unfocused people in all different directions in life.

Read this poem:

One ship drives east another drives west
With the selfsame winds that blow.
'Tis the set of the sails
And not the gales
Which tells us the way to go.

Like the winds of the sea are the winds of fate,
As we voyage along through life,
'Tis the set of the soul
That decides its goal
And not the calm or the strife.

—Ella Wheeler Wilcox

Be enthusiastic, and do the things you don't like doing now, so that later you can do all the things you really enjoy.

What do I like to do?
I like to talk about work, play on tropical beaches, ski at world-class mountain resorts, cash bonus checks, be with friends, things like that.

What don't I like to do?
All the things that allow me to do the things I like.

You will never have to make any difficult decisions as long as you focus on helping other people. Your life's daily decisions will take care of themselves when you pursue a definite major purpose in your life that involves helping others.

To be really successful, you must . . .

Love What You Are Doing

Fall in love with it, or learn to love it. As the old jazz man said, "You've got to love before you can play."

Remember, if you understand and remind yourself *why* you're building your business, then you are 90 percent home free. Woody Allen once said that 80 percent of success in life is "just showing up." That's not enough. 90 percent is knowing *why*. 10 percent of success is knowing *how*. Showing up is required—obviously, but it's not enough. *Why* is the key.

So, what is your purpose?

Whatever *you think* it is—that's what it is. Define it in writing. Get a passion for something in life. Passion drives your purpose—leads it into the future.

And ask yourself these questions:

Where does passion come from? What is the source of passion?

There is only one source of passion: Love.

Get committed to something, your purpose, your dreams, your goals. Commitment to your purpose creates genius, power and magic.

Here is the power of commitment:

Until one is committed there is always hesitancy, the chance to draw back, always ineffectiveness. Concerning all acts of initiative (and creation), there is one elementary truth, the ignorance of which kills countless ideas and splendid plans: that the moment one definitely commits oneself, then Providence moves too. All sorts of things occur to help one that would never otherwise have occurred. A whole stream of events issues from the decision, raising in one's favor all manner of unforeseen incidents and meetings and material assistance, which no man could have dreamt would have come his way.

I have learned a great respect for one of Goethe's couplets;

"Whatever you can do, or dream you can, begin it.
Boldness has genius, power and magic in it."

—W.H. Murray, *The Second Himalayan Expedition*

Clarify your thinking; crystallize exactly the thing you wish to accomplish, and then commit yourself to that goal as your single purpose in life.

Do one thing at a time.

Then go after the next thing.

Goals are the small rewards, the steps to your magnificent dreams and life purpose. A journey of a thousand miles starts with a thought, and then with one step.

Empower others. Enable yourself.

Keep correcting your course, check your goals, reset your goals if you miss. Keep track of your activities. Measure your progress.

Efficiency is doing things right. *Effectiveness* is doing the right things—actions that advance you toward your goals.

Become a teacher of teachers, a trainer of trainers. In Network Marketing, we teach teachers to teach others. It's duplicatable.

Don't go straight for the money. Getting money is not what success is about. The money will be there, but only if you do not focus on it. Helping other people is what success is about.

It's about your freedom: Freedom from debt. Freedom from worry.

Be willing to change your life. Go and grow. Get your dreams and goals down on paper. Then, act boldly as if you could not fail. And never, ever quit!

If entrepreneurs ever adopt a patron saint, it should be the 14th Century Scottish king, Robert the Bruce.

Defeated, discouraged, dejected, Bruce, according to legend, was hiding from his English pursuers on a remote island. Dreamily, he noticed a spider trying painfully to fix its web to a wooden beam. Again and again the creature tried, only to fail each time. But it wouldn't quit. It didn't seem to know how to quit. And in the end it succeeded in building its web.

Leaving his lair, his spirit restored by watching the determined spider, Robert the Bruce gathered a small band of followers and then, against great odds, drove the English out of Scotland.

Robert did not quit.

Will you?

Mentally go into the future. See yourself living the life you want. Work backwards in your imagination, step by step, developing a plan.

Then, take action; move forward knowing you cannot fail. You've seen the future. Never quit until you succeed, and once you achieve success, set new goals. Build a new web.

Tack some pictures on the wall, tape them on the refrigerator, so you'll be constantly reminded of your reasons for building your business.

It's not how you plan your work, it's how you work your plan.

Plan your time, plan your work, but *work your plan.* Follow through with your plan.

Regardless of what might happen.

Regardless of what other people might say.

Regardless of the criticism.

Hang in there with sustained effort, controlled attention and concentrated energy.

Avoid analysis paralysis. Just work your business plan.

You don't need to thoroughly understand a transmission to drive a car. Same thing with your Network Marketing business: just get started and work the system.

Winners never quit.

Quitters never win.

Success is 10 percent conscious brain power, action, sweat, effort, determination, and the unwillingness to quit. The other 90 percent is your subconscious tenacity—the ability to hang onto your dream and keep it in front of you even when it seems impossible to achieve. Success is 90 percent mental toughness and belief.

Make sure they (any of them) don't steal your dream. Forget about the naysayers and prophets of doom who tell you it won't work. Don't listen to the negative opinions and hearsay of uninformed people.

Who are "they," anyway?

They are your peers, your family and your friends.

They don't want you to get hurt.

They don't want you to be more successful than they are.

They don't want you to change, because they are afraid they cannot change.

They don't want you to accomplish anything, because it might make them look bad.

They will hold you back.

They secretly hope you fail, so they will have an excuse not to try to succeed.

They want to say "I told you it wouldn't work." That makes them feel good about themselves.

They are followers with a million reasons why you cannot succeed. They are conformists living lives of mediocrity: complainers. They have a thousand excuses. And you know it's true: When you argue for your excuses and limitations you get to keep them.

Be willing to do the things today that others are unwilling to do, so that someday you can live the lifestyle that others will not have. Do what is hard and necessary now, so you can do what is fun and easy later.

Do what successful people do, learn their habits, duplicate the actions and attitudes of those who are already where you want to be in life, and learn to go against the crowd. Concentrate on creating the attitude and character required for success.

Do the things you need to do, especially when you don't feel like it.

You, too, will be successful, whatever that means for you.

Life is too short to live on someone else's terms.

Those who fail to discipline themselves will submit to the discipline of others.

Those without goals are doomed to work for those who do have goals.

Develop a magnificent obsession for what you want in life. A definite major purpose is the starting point of all achievement.

Plan to win; prepare to win.

Expect to win.

You were born to win.

The secret of success is this: Never, never, ever quit.

Negative responses from uninformed people are 95 percent opinion—not fact.

Never let negative, opinionated people slow you down.

Negative people will steal your dreams—but only if you let them.

When you fly, you feel the incredible power of the jet engines rumbling as the pilot prepares for takeoff. When the brakes are released, the pilot pours full power to the engines down the runway, and he accelerates at 100 percent throttle until the plane reaches its cruising altitude. Then, the pilot pulls back on the throttle, and the engines come down to 80 percent of full power. The plane cruises.

Your business will require 100 percent of your mental effort for it to take off. But once it has taken off and reached a certain altitude, you can pull back on your effort, relax just a little, knowing that the business is cruising and performing safely at 80 percent of maximum effort.

But if you pull back too soon, you'll lose momentum and your business will stall or crash.

Take care.

The 12 Reasons Why People Quit (or Fail to Start)

These are the 12 reasons why people don't succeed.

If you have a challenge in one of these areas, replace the unproductive behavior with goal-achieving actions. Avoid the people who are doing these things. This is the flip side of success, and it's contagious. It isn't fatal, because you can change and replace your behavior.

The following traits describe people who are going nowhere—*stay away from them:*

People don't succeed because . . .

1) They always think they need to do the urgent things first, and they never get around to doing the important things for success.

2) They never decide exactly what they want. They never set any goals.

3) They never take responsibility for their own future. They constantly think and say other people are the cause for their failure. They always blame parents, spouses, kids, bosses, their past, etc.

4) It never occurs to them that they can do more and have more.

5) They never get into action. They never get started. But, they are always talking about what they are going to do tomorrow.

6) They fear failure and are plagued with self-doubt.

7) They fear change, or they have to have status. They think they already are too successful to start something that could make them even more successful. They are afraid to go against the tide of other people, to risk the disapproval of others, to do things differently.

8) They fear success and the responsibility that goes with it. They fear the challenge to remain successful once achieving their initial goals.

9) They fear criticism. They are afraid of what other people might think. They are living the lie, fooling themselves and others that they are doing

well financially when they are not. They are afraid someone will ask them, "If you are doing so well, why do you need this business, too?"

10) They have a spouse who is threatened by any new idea or opportunity. This is fear or status again. The spouse may think, "Oh, not another one. The last thing you tried didn't work out. This won't either."

11) They do not have a long-term perspective on life. They do not know how to delay gratification long enough to get ahead. Short-term thinking causes failure.

12) They fear talking to other people. As children we were told, "Don't talk to strangers." To succeed, a business needs strangers. Strangers are your future customers. A business owner has to talk to new people all the time.

Avoid these 12 hurdles to success. Study and practice the principles of success. Keep your mind focused on what you want. Program your mind to be positive.

Avoid saying, "I can't . . . ." Instead say, "I will . . ."

Stop saying "If . . . ." Instead say, "When . . ."

Anticipate and welcome the changes that life offers you. Seize every opportunity to grow and get better. Take advantage of the situations that other people call problems.

Within every problem lies the seed of a greater opportunity—as you will read in the next chapter.

CHAPTER 10
Choose to Change

W"*here am I trying to go . . . ? And how am I trying to get there . . . ?*" Think about these questions carefully. What's keeping you from serving more people so you can create more volume?

It's *your* future.

Will you be able to pay for the life you want if you don't change something?

You must be willing to change what you are doing now if you want to live differently in the future. Learn how to choose change; learn to welcome it. Most people are where they are in life by accident. Choose your future.

Most people fear change. It's unknown. You'll learn how to get out of your comfort zone, how to relish the feeling of discomfort—temporarily,

You'll learn how to conquer your fear of failure and how to take advantage of change.

You'll learn how to profit from shifting social and economic trends like the following:

"Even if costs rise only five percent a year, four years of private college for today's newborn would run you $128,260 in the year 2008: Four years of public college, $49,094.60."

—USA Today

"If you think your annual tax burden is growing, you are right. The average U.S. taxpayer had to work through the 125th day of this year—two days longer than last year—to satisfy all federal, state, and local tax demands, according to the Tax Foundation. The average worker's tax liability for 1990 equals all of his or her income through May 5,"

—*Nation's Business.*

"In the early 1980s, much of the rise in unemployment came from young workers just entering the labor force, which was growing by roughly two percent annually. Now, the labor force is hardly growing at all, thanks to falling birth rates in the late 1960s and early 1970s. That means that most of the newly jobless are people who have been working for some time and, therefore, have more to lose."

—*Business Week*

"Among aspiring, first-time home buyers, young families in the 25-to-29 age group have been hardest hit. The proportion who own homes has tumbled from 44 percent a decade ago to just over 36 percent today."

—*Fortune*

"The annual survey, done for the International Association for Financial Planning, found 86 percent of households surveyed say severe inflation is likely to be a problem within this decade and 69 percent expect a prolonged recession."

—*USA Today*

"Consumers, meanwhile, have their own set of concerns: disappearing jobs, shrinking incomes, low savings, and high debts. It's not surprising that the Conference Board's index of consumer confidence continued to languish at an eight-year low in December."

—*Business Week*

"Moonlighting is on the rise. A record 7.2 million people—6.2 percent of all workers—have more than one job. That's up from 5.7 million in 1985."

—*USA Today*

"Companies have been laboring to become lean and mean for nearly a decade ... The *Fortune* 500 industrial companies sweated off 3.2 million jobs in the Eighties. Isn't that enough? Not by a long shot. Says Daniel Valentino, president of United Research, a management consulting firm that helps companies restructure: The Eighties were just the tip of the iceberg, and we're going to see dramatic reductions in the Nineties. Corporate America is still as much as 25 percent overstaffed."

—Fortune

The trends identified in these quotes will be with us all through the 1990s and into the 21st century.

Today we are feeling only the tip of the iceberg of phenomenal social and economic changes revealed in those writers' observations. This era of change is as upsetting as it is destined to be long-lasting. It's an historic time, much like when America shifted from the Agricultural Age into an urban society of factory workers in the early part of the 20th century, marking the start of the Industrial Age.

We are undergoing many of the same kinds of changes that came when we became an information-based, technological society during the middle of the 20th century, marking the Information Age.

Today, at the end of the 1990s, we are witnesses to an unprecedented shift in social values and corporate priorities.

Small is okay now.

Efficiency is imperative.

Employee/employer loyalty does not exist.

International perspective is required.

America is becoming a distribution society that is preoccupied with creating volume in a marketplace of products and services.

This is the Distribution Age.

What are you doing to stay ahead of these monumental changes?

How will you take advantage of them?

Will you be able to afford the future—*your future*?

You can either work more hours, make your hours more valuable through increased education and experience, or you can learn to leverage your time.

With more companies striving to be lean and mean—cutting costs by eliminating people and positions—fewer people must work more efficiently to turn out the same or more work.

How secure is *your* paycheck?

When it's time for your company to cut back again, will you survive the ax?

What if you get tossed out in the next round of employee house-cleaning?

Do you have a plan?

You can either cut back your own expenses and trim back your expectations, *or* you can increase your income to match your goals. Your choice.

New jobs are continually being created by new technology, but to participate in them you need new skills, and you may need to relocate.

New jobs created by technology mean old jobs are becoming obsolete fast.

Are you keeping up?

Dual-income families and single-parent families are far more common today. Children go to day care and wait. Mom works because of economic necessity. More kids are working, too. The whole family is working, and there are no more hours to sell.

Is this the kind of family life you want?

With inflation around five percent, a $50,000 income will have to increase to $81,445 in 10 years just to stay even with inflation.

Is "staying even" acceptable for you?

Remember, staying even is staying broke. How will you manage to stay ahead of rising costs?

In the 1980s, the cost of college tuition soared 149 percent.

Will you be able to pay for a college education for your children or yourself?

In the 1980s, the median price of a single-family home jumped 55 percent.
Will you be able to afford a new home?

The costs of airline tickets, hotels, amusements, and restaurants can turn your vacation into more pain than pleasure.
Will you be able to afford the rest and relaxation that you deserve?

Will you be able to afford the so-called "Golden Years," that time in life when you shouldn't have to worry about money or time?
Will you be enjoying your leisure and traveling the world—or will you be worried about money, cutting coupons to finance your next trip to the market?
How will you live when you are in your sixties and older?
You might as well start thinking about it.
Will you cut back on your expectations, spend less, and hope for the best?
Will you stick your head in the sand and deny the obvious economic realities?
Will you pin your hopes on winning a million dollars in the lottery?
Or will you make firm decisions and take action now, realizing that you alone are responsible for creating your own financial future?

You can change your world, including the people in your life, when you change your attitudes and thoughts.
You get back what you give out.
Your outer world is a mirror of your inner world.
You are where you are and what you are as a result of the thoughts you have had.
If you want to live a different life in the future, then you need to change the thoughts you think today. Change by choice, not by chance. Too many

people let the outside world fill their minds with negative thoughts and attitudes.

What's happening in your mind when you listen to radio talk shows, when you listen to music, when you watch television, or when you read the newspaper?

You are filling your mind with attitudes and thoughts—*other people's* attitudes and thoughts—and most of those impressions are *negative.*

When you react to the negative world around you, that's what you create: more negative experience.

When you respond to the world based on your own thoughts, attitudes and expectations, you create the world that you want.

Be aware of the media and other people.

Guard your mind and your attitude against the negative influences that are all around you every day.

Amidst a world of problems, anxieties, fear and anger, you need to create your own reality: a world of beauty, abundance and love.

You create such a world in your mind, in your imagination, and you live your life by your own thoughts and attitudes. The cold, cruel world will still be there. The harsh realities will still be all around you. I'm just saying that you don't have to be affected by them.

When you wake up in the morning, are you excited about having another day, another chance, to get closer to the life you want? Energy and enthusiasm come from wanting something badly and having a financial vehicle for attaining it.

Successful people are excited about life, because they know they are getting closer to the things they want; they keep reaching their goals and setting new ones. They don't care if the sun is shining or if there's a winter storm outside, they know what they want and they know they're going to get it.

That's how you have to live. Lead your life on your own terms.

Take advantage of the changes that are a fact of life. The world around you is always changing. Things happen to people. Things happen that you could not possibly have predicted. Yet, you can remain constant in your mind, with a positive attitude and a solid character. Keeping your future in front of you, constantly doing the things that move you closer to your goals, you do the important things today—not tomorrow.

Focus on the future, not on the past.

Learn from your mistakes in the past, but forget the past.

Dragging your old baggage with you will hold you back.

Be part of the solution, not part of the problem. Look for the good in every situation, and you'll find something good about it. Concentrate on your strengths and learn from everything that happens.

You must be willing to change. Choose to expect and welcome change. Learn to profit from changing social trends. Success is a journey—not a destination.

It is a process. If all you do is cope with the inevitable challenges that come your way and upset your plans and expectations, you will live a life of mediocrity, like all of the complainers.

When you learn to love and anticipate change, treating life as a game, knowing that it's your move and that you are using changes to move forward towards a future of your own design, then you will be inspired by the sudden surprises that come along in life. It's always your move.

View change as a challenge. Every change, every problem, presents to you within itself a greater opportunity, inside the problem is the solution to the problem. Sudden change in your business or your life can be your ally when you take advantage of it.

The way you choose to respond to sudden changes depends on how you have developed your attitude. Welcome the opportunity to change and grow.

Energy and motivation comes from facing changes and setbacks with a positive mental attitude. Look for the seed of a greater opportunity inside every problem. This is easy to do when you have a passion for your goals. When you know what you want and those goals hold a higher priority in your life than the obstacles that come your way, then you will get your major goals. Set many small, easily achievable goals, stepping-stone goals on the way to the really big ones, and remember to reward yourself often.

Successful people do what they say they will do.
They are accountable to themselves and to other people.
They persevere.

Learn to love what you do with a passion. Work hard so that you become excellent at what you do, rather than simply for material gain. When you love doing something you will become excellent at it, you will be successful—and you will get your goals.

What are some of the social and economic changes that we will all be facing in the coming years? Will you use them to move ahead and stay ahead? And how will you use them . . . ?

1) INCREASED TRAFFIC GRIDLOCK AND RESTRICTED USE OF PRIVATE CARS.
The San Francisco Chronicle polled its readers and identified traffic gridlock as the number one concern. Another study predicts that in the coming years traffic will be moving 50 percent slower in most major commute areas. If you spend an hour on the road driving to work now, plan to double it.

The New York Times says we will be priced out of our cars. We will endure increased bridge tolls, pay-by-the-mile toll roads, increased vehicle registration, increased gas taxes, increased parking fees, and increased time on the road.

If you depend on driving your car to earn your income, you need to develop an alternate source of income.

2) DECREASING JOB SECURITY IN THE WORKPLACE.
It is well understood today that the implied commitments of employer-employee loyalty do not exist anymore. There is no lifetime employment for people with a job.

3) EXPLOSIVE GROWTH OF ENTREPRENEURS AND HOME-BASED BUSINESSES.

More people are responding to the traffic and the lack of job security by starting their own businesses. Many get started part-time with little time and money involved. By giving up television and some of the other unproductive activities that do not contribute to your future and your goals, you will have several hours a day and more on weekends to build your business.

4) INCREASED INTEREST IN LIVING AT A SLOWER PACE WITH MORE TIME.

Baby-boomers are slowing down and they are sending a message to the rest of society. The boomers realized that you cannot race around and try to have it all and still enjoy a quality, balanced life. A status symbol for mothers is to be able to afford to give up the career and to devote time and energy to the home. There is a widespread pursuit of a slower, meaningful life with balance in all areas of life—and that means having more time.

5) EXPLOSIVE GROWTH OF AT-HOME SHOPPING AND A RESURGENCE OF HOME DELIVERY.

In the spirit of saving time, more people are choosing to shop from home by telephone, computer or television. Especially for basic consumer goods, people are ordering the easiest way possible and having the products delivered to their home.

6) GROWTH OF WAREHOUSE AND WHOLESALE SHOPPING.

For fresh foods and many consumer items, more people are shopping at Walmart, Price Club, Costco, Sam's Club, Factory Outlets, and other wholesale warehouse stores. Status-conscious boomers are not afraid to be seen at a cut-rate, wholesale outlet to buy the basics. They are saving money any way they can.

7) CONTINUED SURGE IN POPULARITY AND SUPPORT FOR ENVIRONMENTALLY-SAFE PRODUCTS, PACKAGING AND BUSINESS PRACTICES.

More people say it is important to shop "green." Increased attention is being given to health in general—a healthy planet, healthy environment, healthy body and mind.

Recycling is big business today. The International Chamber of Commerce in Paris reports a major trend of businesses turning "green" globally.

Americans, too, have changed their purchasing decisions based on concerns about the environment:

- Five percent find a company's environmental reputation is important in deciding which brands to buy, and would pay more for biodegradable and recyclable containers.

- 56 percent refused to buy a product during the past year because of environmental concerns

- 94 percent see buying products in environmentally-sound packaging as one solution to consumer solid waste problems.

8) DECREASED EFFECTIVENESS OF MASS MEDIA ADVERTISING.
With more television channels and radio stations via cable and satellite transmission, no company can afford to dominate the audience the way they could when there were only three primary channels. Mass advertising is losing its power to influence people, because we have become a very sophisticated audience, and it takes more than video flash and dazzle to impress us. We are suspicious and we don't believe their claims anymore.

Mass advertising is too expensive today for most companies to run enough ads to affect very many people. Major firms are finding ways to cut back on expenses, especially on ad campaigns where they can't even prove if the ads are working.

There is a significant trend toward finding alternate ways to get products and company names in front of consumers. It's a movement "back to basics" and towards creating word of mouth and person-to-person marketing with fresh approaches.

The best-selling book, *50 Things You Can Do to Save the Earth,* recommends as its number one strategy to *stop junk mail.*

A direct mail revolution is growing out here in the ranks of mass mail recipients. Almost 1.5 million people have requested the Direct Marketing

Association to delete their names from all mailing lists, and the requests are increasing at the rate of 50,000 a month.

Many people in the workplace and at home consider direct mail advertising to be a time waster and a resource waster, and they resent it. Junk telephone calls are their next targets.

9) STEADY GROWTH OF INTERNATIONAL BUSINESS EXPANSION IN LATIN AMERICA AND IN THE ASIAN-PACIFIC RIM COUNTRIES.

Political borders are coming down. Trade barriers are disappearing. The world economy is becoming a reality. International marketing is required for a company to grow.

The Asian-Pacific Rim market will rival or exceed the U.S. and European markets by the year 2000 for many products and industries. The most successful U.S. companies in the Pacific Rim are IBM, CocaCola, Amway, Johnson & Johnson, Proctor and Gamble, Clinique, McDonalds and Motorola.

10) GROWTH OF DIVERSIFIED, MULTIPLE INCOME FAMILIES, NOT DUAL INCOMES.

It is common for ambitious people to be running a business from their homes or from small offices, in addition to holding down a job.

More couples are working together in home-based businesses while one or both of them continues to pursue a career, in anticipation of the day when their business grows to the point where they don't need to depend on the job and salary.

11) GROWTH OF NETWORK MARKETING AS AN ACCEPTED, POPULAR WAY TO BUILD A LARGE BUSINESS.

Network Marketing companies offer entrepreneurs a way to capitalize on all of the changes listed above.

A successful, home-based, no-limit, Network Marketing business solves the traffic headaches of commuting to a job.

It removes the financial insecurity of depending on a job.

It offers the opportunity to build a very large business without the need for large time and money commitments in the beginning.

It allows couples to be together; it allows families to spend more time together on a daily basis.

A Network Marketing business can offer extensive catalogs of consumer products at wholesale prices that can be ordered from home by phone or computer and delivered to the home in two to three days.

Many Network Marketing companies offer complete lines of environmentally-safe, cruelty-free consumer products.

A Network Marketing business does not require mass advertising; it is a classic word-of-mouth, person-to-person business.

Many Network Marketing companies have expanded all over the world, and so it is possible for your Network Marketing business to grow into 60 or 70 countries today—without the need to ever leave town.

A Network Marketing business offers families a way to diversify their income, over and above what they already earn.

It is an opportunity to create another source of income on a part-time basis.

And for an increasing number of men, women and families, Network Marketing is an opportunity to create a richly rewarding career where you earn the money to have what you want—and the time to enjoy your life to the fullest.

What Is Important to People Today?

a) Personal service
b) Convenience
c) Quality
d) Making a contribution to others

All the things that Network marketing offers.

More people are getting involved in helping others through community service. They are keeping a low profile, and they are unloading personal debt.

Debt-free is stress-free.

The goal for more and more people in the 90s is to get rid of consumer debt. It marks the end of the card-charging yuppies. Urban professionals may still be around in the 1990s with money to spend and influence to spare—but they are neither upwardly mobile nor all that young anymore.

Aging baby-boomers have spawned a newly sobered, thrifty, family-oriented generation. They want more than a flashy car and the best seat in the house. They want traditional values. They have found that a life based on materialism is not satisfying.

Putting It Together—A Quick Review

Choose to be excited about life, and influence other people with your enthusiasm.

Develop a burning desire inside you for your dream.

Get your goals no matter what, so long as you don't violate the rights of other people and the universal laws of nature.

Own the most powerful business idea available: a Network Marketing business.

Learn to leverage your time and *own your future.*

Develop residual income.

Diversify your income.

Set up your modern home-based business.

Make full use of the tax advantages.

Learn to develop depth in your business. Network Marketing is the only business concept where you can develop unlimited depth in your business. In business as usual, depth comes from referrals, but referrals cannot be duplicated—they happen mostly by accident.

Do not commute. Do not depend on your car for your income.

Profit from the growing trends in wholesale buying.

Cash in on at-home shopping and home delivery.

Get involved with a company that has environmentally sound products, packaging, and business practices.

Find your opportunity in the consumer market. Get involved in the distribution of products and services that people need and buy every week, every month.

Develop a balanced concept of success in the six important areas of your life:

1) Spiritual
2) Family
3) Social
4) Mental
5) Physical
6) Financial

Set specific goals and keep them in front of you at all times.
Build an international business.

You can own a business that fits all of these parameters. And you can build a successful business part-time without threatening your current financial situation.

You now have all of the information that you need.

The question is:

How badly do you want your goals? Badly enough?

And here's another question:

What are your other options?

If you don't build a Network Marketing business, what are you going to do?

There's no such thing in life as standing still.

You either grow, or you wither away.

And it's a lot more fun to grow.

The more people you talk to, the more successful you'll be. Stretch outside your comfort zone. If you are a little uncomfortable, that's good: you are growing, that's where you should be.

Just talk to people.

Learn to relax.

Smile.

Laugh.

Learn to talk to anybody.

As little kids, we were warned not to talk to strangers. Forget that! You need to talk to strangers now.

The only way to learn how is to start doing it. It doesn't matter if you're no good at it at first; nobody was ever any good at it, at first. Just keep doing it; it's the only way to get better.

Start by saying, "Hi" to people. Smile when you say it. Be friendly. You'll get back what you give out.

Talk to other people for those you've sponsored into your business. Ask questions that show you are interested in them. Get your eyes off of yourself. Become a listener. Most people talk too much. You cannot learn anything when you are talking.

We have two ears and one mouth. Do you suppose that means that we should listen twice as much as we talk? Makes sense to me. And it works. Get the other person to do most of the talking. They'll think you are a terrific conversationalist. When you listen to people, you will find out what they want. Then you can show them a way to get the things they want.

Ask questions that are open-ended, that encourage further conversation—not questions that elicit a simple "Yes" or "No" answer.

Ask, "How do you mean?" or "Can you tell me more about that?"

Rephrase people's statements or questions in a question of your own, to make sure you understand them. Be a caring, intent listener, with a genuine, sincere interest in people. You will discover their interests and their dreams, and you can show them a way to get their dreams.

Offer them a million-dollar business that they can start for a few hundred dollars and a little bit of time. You have your hands on a valuable opportunity for success—arguably, the very best opportunity in the world!

Seek out excellence in people. Find a mentor, a leader who is where you want to be in life. Someone who can and will help you get there, too.

Become a mentor for others.

Dress sharp for success. Learn to be irresistible with an attractive personality. You make 40 impressions in the first minute when you meet someone. First impressions count. You never get a second chance to make a first impression.

Become a student of people. Learn "people skills."

Become a mirror and reflect back their physical posture and their tone of voice. Learn to pace the other person. If they talk fast, you talk fast. If they talk slow, slow down.

We like people who are like us. When you become like someone else, you create rapport. You are not giving up your personality or being phony; you are eliminating the obvious differences between you, and that helps to create a meeting of the minds. This is something we do unconsciously anyway; just become conscious of it, and learn to do it better and more often. Matching the other person creates an environment without distractions, and the other person can concentrate on your ideas and thoughts, rather than being distracted by the personal differences between you.

Learn to think and talk like the person you are talking with, and you will have a better chance of communicating. Reflect them back to themselves.

Some people are visual thinkers. They see the world in pictures. They use phrases like, "I see what you mean," or, "That looks like a good idea."

Other people are auditory thinkers. They hear the world in sounds. They use phrases like, "I hear what you're saying," or "That sounds like a good idea."

Others process the world from an kinesthetic point of view. Their world is filled with feelings. They use phrases like, "I have the feeling this will work," or "I get the sense that you have a good grasp of the idea."

You can identify the way a person is processing the world at that precise moment in time. We use all three methods of thinking, and we switch back and forth, but most of us have a dominant mode that we stick with. Figure out which one a person is using, and switch into that mode, so you can relate more closely and create rapport.

There are four different personality styles, and when you recognize another person's style, you have another opportunity to create deeper rapport and greater communication.

1) Driver

These people want to control other people and circumstances. They put great emphasis on results and on the bottom line. They are impatient and loud. They tend to get things done, even if they have to do it themselves. They don't care if they make someone angry, and they tend to move and talk fast.

2) Amiable

These people want to be liked by everyone. They avoid situations that create conflict. They are more concerned with relationships than with results. They are very patient, and they don't want to make anyone angry. They are nice and easy to get along with. They are peacemakers.

3) Expressive

These people will talk all day. You'll find them in groups of other people. They chatter. They are outgoing and generous. They are story tellers, and they seem to have hundreds of friends. They are emotional and they wear their feelings on the outside. They are easy to talk to and easy to get to know. They'll probably do all the talking. They are not concerned with details; they relish the ongoing process of a project.

4) Analytical

These people want to know all the details. Sometimes, they get accused of suffering from "paralysis by analysis." They would rather have all the information than the results. They need to know where every cent went. They have to cover all of the "what ifs" before they make a move. They will study something to death. They want to know everything about how it works first. They sometimes seem to make little or no progress on a project.

Which style are you?

A combination of two or three, probably. Most of us have a dominant personality style.

When you are with someone, you want to create rapport and communication. Identify which is their dominant personality style, and match it.

Reach out to people.
Give away yourself and your business.
Invest your time in other people.

Remember, everything rubs off. Everything counts. Every minute counts. Focus on your priorities.
Everything grows.

Avoid negative people. Be around positive people.
Be around people who have the success and the life you want.

Inspire people and let others inspire you.

Motivation wears off. Keep reading. Keep learning.

Keep your dreams and goals in front of you.
Priorities, priorities, priorities!
Get your goal no matter what.

Learn to do the basics of the business, and do them over and over and over ...

This is the enthusiasm business; it's not a matter of hype—you simply have to be sold yourself.
Give your enthusiasm away to other people. The more you give away, the more you'll have. Enthusiasm is a spirit within you. Keep it alive.
Make your business a labor of love.

Save 10 percent of your income for the future.

Invest 10 percent of your time for the future.

You will become wealthy both in time and money.

This is not the convincing business. It is a business of sorting people.

Find the ambitious, open-minded, positive ones who want more out of life.

Stop convincing; start sorting and sharing.

Keep your business simple so others can duplicate it.

Follow the Eight-Step Success System and work on yourself.

Work your business on faith for one year without looking back.

Your business will explode.

You will be free.

We'll see you at the top with the winners in life.

We'll look for you on the beaches of the world, having fun and enjoying life.

Your Network Marketing business will keep growing.

You will be able to take off a week or a year to pursue other interests.

Your income will not be affected. The money will keep coming.

It's true.

It's residual income—the finest kind!

CHAPTER 11
Recommended Books and Tapes

Readers are leaders. Leaders are readers. And they listen to tapes every chance they get, too. Reading and thinking are to the mind what exercise and oxygen are to the body.

When you read at least 15 minutes a day in books that can help you grow, and when you turn your car into a rolling university by listening to cassette tapes instead of music, you will find yourself dreaming bigger and getting your goals more quickly, one after another after another.

You will be *Getting A Life* all the time. You'll be growing and expanding—all the time.

The books and tapes listed in this chapter will help you to become success conscious and success aware. The principles for achieving happiness and success today are the same principles that King Solomon used to create his vast fortune in 966 B.C.

Success principles do not change.

You can learn to use these principles, too. You can rely on them and trust in them.

The following list of books and audio tapes contains some of the classic literature in the field of success principles.

Many of the writers now sound a bit old-fashioned, or perhaps overly formal in their expression—and some, sadly, did not anticipate that many of their readers would be women. So, forgive them if it seems as if they are writing for men only.

There are many more books and tapes available than the selection on this list, and after you have read the books recommended here, you will want to keep reading in the field, exploring on your own, discovering new ones and other classics not listed here. What's more, new ones, good ones are appearing all the time.

Personal Leadership and Self-Development Books

The following books are available in most libraries and bookstores and through a number of catalogs and organizations serving the Network Marketing industry.

A Better Way To Live, Og Mandino; Bantam Books. Seventeen rules to live by for inner growth and fulfillment.

Acres of Diamonds, Russell H. Conwell; Jove Books, 1978. A world-famous and classic story.

Ageless Body, Timeless Mind, Deepak Chopra; Harmony Books, 1993. A quantum alternative to growing old.

An Uncommon Freedom, Charles Paul Conn; Berkley Books, 1986. The Amway experience and why it grows.

As a Man Thinketh, James Allen; Grosset and Dunlap. A 1800s classic of words to guide you.

Autobiography of Benjamin Franklin, Ben Franklin; Macmillan Publishing, 1962. An American original.

Be a Motivational Leader, Leroy Eims; Victor Books, 1989. Learn to be an effective leader.

Being The Best, Denis Waitley; Simon & Schuster, 1988. A life-changing guide to real success, winning at life.

Believe!, Richard M. DeVos and Charles Paul Conn; Berkley Books, 1985. Old-fashioned, durable principles are the foundation of success.

Blueprints For Memory, William D. Hersey; Amacon, 1990. How to remember facts, figures and faces.

Bringing Out The Best In People, Alan McGinnis; Augsburg Publishing, 1985. Learn life's greatest joy, helping others to grow.

Change Your Voice, Change Your Life, Dr. Morton Cooper; Harper and Row, 1985. A quick, simple plan for finding and using your natural dynamic voice.

Confidence, How To Succeed At Being Yourself, Alan Loy McGinnis; Augsburg Publishing House, 1987. A book to help you succeed by being yourself.

Creating Affluence, Deepak Chopra, MD; New World Library, 1993. The best of Eastern and Western thought combined, ancient wisdom and modern science.

Creating Health, Deepak Chopra, MD; Houghton Mifflin Co., 1987. The reality beyond current ideas about health and illness.

Double Win, Denis Waitley; Berkley Books, 1986. How to get to the top without putting others down.

Enthusiasm Makes The Difference, Norman Vincent Peale; Ballantine Books, 1988. How to be vital, alive and a winner.

Essence Of Success, Earl Nightingale; Nightingale Conant Corp., 1993. 163 life lessons from the dean of self-improvement.

Executive Memory Techniques, Jon Keith; Dell Trade Paperback, 1989. Train your memory for self-confidence, self-esteem and success.

Flow, Mihaly Csikszentinihalyi; Harper & Row, 1990. A summary of decades of research on the positive aspects of human experience.

Friendship Factor, Alan Loy McGinnis; Augsburg Publishing House, 1979. A warmly written, practical guide to human relationships.

Get The Best From Yourself, Nido R. Qubein; Berkley Books, 1986. A proven formula for personal and professional success.

Getting To Yes, Roger Fisher and William Ury; Penguin Book, 1987. How to negotiate agreement without giving in.

Go Getter, Peter B. Kyne; Holt Rinehart & Winston, 1949. A classic story that tells you how to be a go-getter.

Greatest Miracle In The World, Og Mandino; Bantam Books, 1988. Exciting, insightful secrets for personal happiness and success.

Greatest Networker In The World, John Milton Fogg; Upline™ Press/MLM Publishing, Inc., 1992. A most inspiring story that shows you "who to be" for success in Network Marketing.

Greatest Opportunity In The History Of The World, John Kalench; MIM Publications, 1991. The history and "whys" of taking a look at Network Marketing.

Greatest Salesman In The World, Og Mandino; Bantam Books, 1988. The master story-teller's first book. A classic work.

Greatest Secret In The World, Og Mandino; Bantam Books, 1988. How to unlock a world of personal happiness.

Grow Rich With Peace Of Mind, Napolean Hill; Ballantine Books, 1967. Earn the money you need and enrich every part of your life.

How To Build A Better Vocabulary, Maxwell Nurnberg and Morris Rosenblum; Warner Books, 1989. Have fun building your vocabulary.

How To Be Rich, J. Paul Getty; Jove Books, 1983. Wealth formulas from the legend himself.

How To Win Friends And Influence People, Dale Carnegie; Pocket Books, 1981. Classic, time-tested and rock-solid advice; the original.

How To Have Confidence And Power In Dealing With People, Les Giblin; Prentice Hall In., 1986. Learn to work with human nature—not against it.

How To Stop Worrying And Start Living, Dale Carnegie; Pocket Books, 1985. Time-tested methods to conquer doubt and worry.

I Dare You, William H. Danforth; Privately published, 1988. Dare to be your best and serve others.

In Search Of Excellence, Thomas J. Peters and Robert H. Waterman, Jr.; Warner Books, 1984. Lessons from America's best-run companies.

Law Of Success, Napolean Hill; Success Unlimited, 1992. His original book based on 20 years of research.

Life Is Tremendous, Charlie "Tremendous" Jones; Living Books, 1968. Enthusiasm makes the difference.

Living With Passion, Peter L. Hirsch; Upline™ Press/MLM Publishing, Inc., 1994. Ten simple secrets that guarantee your success.

Love Is The Answer, Gerald G. Jampolsky, MD and Diane V. Cirincione; Bantam Books, 1990. On creating positive relationships

Magic Of Believing, Claude M. Bristol; Simon & Schuster, 1969. Learn to release powerful forces locked in your mind.

Magic Of Getting What You Want, David J. Schwartz, Ph.D.; Berkley Book, 1984. The magic of creative dreaming.

Magic Of Thinking Big, David J. Schwartz, Ph.D.; Prentice Hall, 1959. A classic book: a planned program for living on a grand scale.

Magic Of Thinking Success, David J. Schwartz, Ph.D.; Wilshire Book Co., 1987. A personal guide to financial independence.

Master Your Money, Ron Blue; Thomas Nelson Publishers, 1986. A step-by-step plan for financial freedom.

Maximum Achievement, Brian Tracy; Simon & Schuster, 1993. Proven strategies and skills that will unlock your hidden powers to succeed.

Megatrends, John Naisbitt; Warner Books, 1984. The first book to predict the phenomenon of Networking.

Megatrends 2000, John Naisbitt and Patricia Aburdene; William Morrow & C., 1990. Round two of the *Megatrends* saga.

Mission Success, Og Mandino; Bantam Books, 1987. A personal message of hope and happiness for a successful life.

Money Money Money Money Money, John Milton Fogg; *Upline*™ Press/MLM Publishing, Inc., 1994. An ultra-quick, persuasive little read on why you should get involved in your own Network Marketing business.

Move Ahead With Possibility Thinking, Robert H. Schuller; Jove Books, 1978. A practical, easy-to-follow program for possibilities.

New Dynamics Of Winning, Denis Waitley; Morrow & C., 1993. How to gain the mind set of a champion.

One Minute Manager, Spencer Johnson, M.D. and Kenneth Blanchard, Ph.D.; Berkley Books, 1982. A quick way to increase your own professional value and personal prosperity.

Overnight Guide To Public Speaking, Ed Wohlmuth; Running Press 1983. A six-step system for mastering the lectern.

Path Of Least Resistance, Robert Fritz; Ballantine Books, 1984. Learning to become the dominant creative force in your own life.

Positive Imaging, Norman Vincent Peale; Ballantine Books, 1990. A master method for overcoming worry, loneliness and disease.

Positive Addiction, William Glasser, MD; Harper & Row, 1976. How to gain strength and self-esteem through positive behavior.

Possible Dream, Charles Paul Conn; Berkley Books, 1978. A candid insider's look at Amway.

Power Of Optimism, Alan Loy McGinnis; Harper & Row, 1990. How to become a more optimistic person.

Power Of Positive Thinking, Norman Vincent Peale; Prentice Hall, 1984. One of the greatest inspirational books ever.

Promises To Keep, Charles Paul Conn; Berkley Books, 1992. More on the Amway phenomenon and how it works.

Psychocybernetics, Maxwell Maltz, MD, F.I.C.S.; Prentice Hall, 1960. Using subconscious power and self-image psychology to influence your life.

Psychology Of Winning, Denis Waitley; Berkley Books, 1984. 10 qualities of a total winner.

Quick And Easy Way To Effective Speaking, Dale Carnegie; Simon & Schuster, 1977. Techniques for dynamic communication.

Raising Positive Kids In A Negative World, Zig Ziglar; Ballantine Books, 1989. A step-by-step prescription for success with your kids.

Real Magic, Dr. Wayne W. Dyer; Harper Collins, 1992. How to create real miracles in everyday life.

Richest Man In Babylon, George S. Clason; Signet, 1988. The success secrets of the ancients; a true classic.

See You At The Top, Zig Ziglar; Pelican Publishing, 1990. Improve your performance by changing the way you think about yourself.

Seeds Of Greatness, Denis Waitley; Simon & Schuster, 1984. The ten best-kept secrets of total success.

Self Talk Solution, Shad Helmstetter; Pocket Books, 1987. A proven, self-management program for success.

Seven Habits Of Highly Effective People, Stephen R. Covey; Simon & Schuster, 1989. A study of the past 200 years of success literature.

17 Secrets Of The Master Prospectors, John Kalench; MIM Publications, 1994. The secrets to master the life's blood of successful Network Marketing.

$treet $mart Networking, Robert Butwin; MLM Publishing, Inc. 1994. Practical, proven, powerful "how tos" from a real Networking success story.

Success, The Glenn Bland Method, Glenn Bland; Living Books, 1972. How to set goals and make plans that really work.

Success Through A Positive Mental Attitude, Napolean Hill and W. Clement Stone; Simon & Schuster, 1987. A world-famous book that could be worth millions to you.

Swim With Sharks Without Being Eaten Alive, Harvey Mackay; Ivy Books, 1990. Straight from the hip handbook by a self-made millionaire.

The Art Of Public Speaking, Ed McMahon; Ballantine Books, 1986. America's Toastmaster shares secrets of public speaking success.

The Art Of Talking So People Will Listen, Paul W. Swets; Prentice Hall, 1983. Getting through to family, friends and business associates.

The Art Of The Leader, William A. Coher, Ph.D.; Prentice Hall, 1990. Understanding the qualities which combined create an effective leader.

The Choice, Og Mandino; Bantam Books, 1988. The key to a freer, richer future. (Some say it's his best.)

The Leader In You, Stuart R. Levine and Michael A. Crom; Simon Schuster, 1983. How to win friends, influence people, and succeed in a changing world.

The Success System That Never Fails, W. Clement Stone; Simon Schuster, 1980. How to develop your own blueprint for success.

Think And Grow Rich, Napolean Hill; Fawcett Crest, 1960. THE classic. Money-making secrets that can change your life.

Top Performance, Zig Ziglar; Berkley Books, 1987. How to develop excellence in yourself and others.

Tough Minded Optimist, Norman Vincent Peale; Prentice Hall, 1989. An effective approach to mastering the challenges of living today.

True Believer, Eric Hoffa; Harper & Row, 1989. Thoughts on the nature of mass movements.

University Of Success, Og Mandino; Bantam Books, 1982. Fifty renowned experts present a complete course on how to succeed.

Unlimited Power, Anthony Robbins; Ballantine Books, 1989. The new science of personal achievement.

Voice Power, Joan Kenley, Ph.D.; Henry Holt & Co., 1989. A breakthrough method to enhance your speaking voice.

What To Say When You Talk To Yourself, Shad Helmstetter, Ph.D.; Pocket Books, 1982. Powerful techniques to program your potential for success.

Who Stole The American Dream—The book your boss doesn't want you to read, Burke Hedges; INTI, 1992. Why Network Marketing is such a powerful answer to the dilemma of today's disappearing employment opportunities.

Winner's Circle, Charles Paul Conn; Berkley Books, 1979. Personal stories of Network Marketing's most successful company's most successful distributors.

You And Your Network, Fred Smith; Key Word Books, 1984. How to get the most out of your life.

You Can Become The Person You Want To Be, Robert H. Schuller; Jove Books, 1984. Self-confidence, getting and keeping it.

The following are audiotape programs (typically six-tape sets). These audio tape sets are available from various retail outlets, mail-order catalogs and direct from the publisher: Nightingale/Conant, 800-525-900 Chicago, Illinios.

Flextactics, Denis Waitley
Getting Rich In America, Brian Tracy
Goals, Zig Ziglar
Higher Self, Deepak Chopra, M.D., F.I.S.C.
How to Be a No-Limit Person, Dr. Wayne W. Dyer
How to Master Your Time, Brian Tracy
Lead The Field, Earl Nightingale
Leadership, Kenneth Blanchard, Ph.D. and Brian Tracy
Magical Mind, Magical Body, Deepak Chopra
New Dynamics Of Winning, Denis Waitley

Power Persuasion, Roger Dawson
Psychology of Achievement, Brian Tracy
Psychology of Success, Brian Tracy
Psycho-Cybernetics, Maxwell Maltz, M.D., F.I.S.C.
Science of Personal Achievement, Napolean Hill
Science of Self Confidence, Brian Tracy
Secrets of Power Negotiating, Roger Dawson
Strangest Secret, Earl Nightingale
Success Through a Positive Mental Attitude, Napolean Hill and
    W. Clement Stone
Successful Communicator, Earl Nightingale
Think and Grow Rich, Napolean Hill
Universal Laws of Success and Achievement, Brian Tracy
Your Right To Be Rich, Napolean Hill